Jaybyrd

The Hermit of Sycamore Canyon

Eileen Moore

Author's Note

In 2018, I was working on Arizona Springs: The Desert's Draught. The book included a chapter on the hermits that depended on the springs for water. As I interviewed Jay, I recognized his story was more than just a song to the springs and suggested I write about his life. Jay started texting book titles to me. Unfortunately, he died before the manuscript was completed. Jay's friends have been very generous in answering my questions and this book has come to print. Any errors in the account are either mine or a difference in memory between two sources. I regret any misunderstanding. The fact remains that Jay was a very unusual man, rich in God's grace. His story is one of redemption and the decision to make a U-turn in life, away from darkness into light.

Jaybyrd: The Hermit of Sycamore Canyon
Eileen Moore

Published by Morten Moore Publishers
415 E. Mohawk
Flagstaff, AZ 86005

Copyright Ruth Mortenson 2021
ISBN 978-0-9991108-8-1

Jaybyrd

The Hermit of Sycamore Canyon

O beata solitudo,
O sola beatitudo.

O blessed solitude
only happiness.

Have you ever longed to run away from life? Have you dreamed of starting over when your circumstances became too painful?

As a teenager, I would lie in bed in the evening, dreaming of running away to live in the mountains of Colorado. My home was filled with tension. I came to the point one evening of crouching on the window ledge, plotting my escape through the lemon tree that stood outside the window.

But, I turned back and sank into bed. I thought of walking through the dark streets to the bus station. What did a bus ticket to Colorado cost? Could I find a wreck of a small cabin to restore as a shelter? Maybe it would be within walking distance of a small town where I could find a job to buy food and supplies. How would I deal with the winter snow? Would I find sufficient shelter?

These thoughts sifted through my mind as I drifted off to sleep. I was not the first or the last teenager to dream of running away to live, isolated from society with no rules or expectations. To my point, just witness the popularity of the book, *My Side of the Mountain*.

The choice to leave the world we know behind and escape the pressures of society is one that stretches back for centuries. Stories of men becoming hermits have found a home in our urban legends. But like the teenager I once was, wrapped in the security of our civilized life, few are willing to sacrifice the comfort offered by social interaction for the solitary existence.

I know one man who became a hermit, of sorts. Or maybe we could call him a mystic as his choice to live alone centered on his quest to seek what was true and of eternal worth. He wasn't cut out in the role of an ancient anchorite. If anything, he was a practical-minded man choosing to live apart from the distractions of life.

In 2018, I interviewed Jay Willison for a book on the springs of Arizona. We had become friends through his involvement with a ministry at the local jail. This was a man I would not have easily come to know in my everyday routine. My husband and I found him to be a person who accepted us for who we were despite the differences between us. After Jay's death, we repeatedly heard the same from others: "Jay met me where I was at."

As I began to write about his days living in the Sycamore Canyon Wilderness, I realized I could never tell the story of his amazing transformation from drug dealing law-breaker to quotidian mystic in one short chapter. His tale required a small book. I thought I would fill in many of the details in future conversations with him. Before I could ask questions to fill in the gaps of my basic outline, Jay reached the end of his days. This story is based on my interview with him and interviews with some of his friends. I wish it were more complete but even with this limited accounting, you will come to understand that what happened to Jay leaves many of us asking questions about what we value and what is true.

Scrounge Sculpture / Jaybyrd

Part One

Jaybyrd

Chapter 1

Jay was born in 1953 in Southern California. In the early 1950s, Los Angeles was like a glutton reeling after a heavy meal from the war-time industries of World War II. The Korean Conflict had created a demand for war materials but the industry was slowing down and cracks were beginning to appear in a culture bred by the deprivation of the 1930s.

The culture of the US in the 1950's was based on the nuclear family: The father as the head of the family, the mother caring for the children at home. During World War II, many women had worked in the war industries in the 1940s. Now, the men had returned and our culture was facing some serious challenges. The Willison family, with Jay, settled into North Hollywood, a community of modest neighborhoods and small businesses on the southern edge of the prosperous San Fernando Valley. To the south, Burbank and Pasadena retained the image of golden California but North Hollywood had begun to slide into the bleak gray of a city built along streams of asphalt.

Harley Davidson recognized the desire to escape the terrible conflict in the the men returning from the war. The company cultivated the image of a young rebel breaking free from the constraints of society. Be like James Dean, hop on a bike and shrug off the rules. Many young boys still dreamed of being a firefighter or a policeman but Jay admired the men roaring through the streets of North Hollywood on loud Harleys. These wanna-be outlaws became his heros.

As the biker culture evolved, this image of escaping the restrictions of society evolved into the outlaw biker gangs. Jay was fascinated, drawn to the outlaw biker image. Hair flying free, legs clad in denim, the riders wheeled through traffic as if they were flying. They seemed free, unbound by the working grind. Jay became determined to follow his own path as he grew up.

His father was a hard-bitten, no nonsense veteran who had his own ideas about escape from the grim streets of the big city. Jay described his dad as a man who loved the outdoors. A man who excelled in the outdoor crafts from building a fire to hunting for dinner. He hated the streets of North Hollywood.

Jay's mom leaned toward Wiccan practices. One friend describes Jay as "a man born into a loveless marriage with two very flawed people who lived day-to-day with little thought beyond their routine." The strain of making a living with two active boys wore at the bond of marriage until the bond severed.

To support her family, his mom found a job and Jay became a latchkey kid. When school let out, he wandered the streets, turning at the sound of a loud motor, to watch a blue jean-clad biker with long hair and fringe jacket glide by on the street.

All too soon, men hanging around the light posts began to watch the tall, skinny kid who haunted the streets. They nodded as he passed and Jay was drawn into their conversations. He listened to the slang of the streets and understood their activities were not always lawful. In those days of watching and listening, Jay understood that he could sit quietly and learn more than was being said in a conversation. He learned to read the body language of those around him.

The day came when he tagged along with an older kid to a small market. The kid slipped a pack of cigarettes into his back pocket, allowing a loose fitting shirt to slide down, disguising the bulge. Jay found it easy to sell the pack for a couple of bucks on the street.

Within weeks he followed the kid into a neighborhood of homes with clean streets and green yards. They slipped through a backyard fence and jimmied a window. Sliding into the quiet home, they sifted through the family's possessions for anything valuable. Out the back, the boys met two men who paid them for the small items they had found. Jay fingered the bills in his pocket. So easy! A quick way to pick up some spending money.

Two years later, he held down a street corner. As he nimbly plucked a bill from a client's hand, a hand gripped his shoulder. Jay found himself in the back of a patrol car, handcuffs binding his wrists. He was on his way to Juvenile Court.

In detention, Jay learned more of the skills of a professional thief. He learned to case a neighborhood. He observed which homes had cars parked in the driveway or showed

A reflective pose high on a mountain; Jay's father.

evidence of a woman in the house. Was there a dog in the back yard? A gate in the fence? He looked over the barrier and examined each window. Were any windows open or could he jimmy a lock to allow a soundless entry? Breaking the glass made noise. He learned the places a homeowner hid cash or valuables. He heard minutes ticking off as he remained in the home, searching for valuables. The longer he remained inside a home, the higher the risk of being caught. He chose to become a professional thief, taking others' possessions and selling them to a pawn shop or on the streets.

His mother sent him to a professional counselor, hoping he would turn away from criminal activity. Eventually, she pronounced an ultimatum. Either Jay could live on the streets or he could live with his dad in Oregon. She had tried her best to shape him into a responsible young man but the streets seem more appealing. Jay chose to live with his father.

Looking back, Jay shook his head. "I gave my family a lot of grief!"

His brother, Brady stayed with his mom for a time. Brady looked up to his older brother but Jay was not interested in being a role model. The brothers began to take separate paths through life. Jay might have influenced Brady to pursue a better course in life but the brothers often fought and Jay was consumed by his own pursuits. By age 13, Brady had his own run-in with law enforcement.

When Jay joined his father's new family, his dad thought he might benefit from time spent in the woods, camping and fishing. Jay admired his dad's woods craft including his ability to set up a shelter. His dad taught him the forests were valuable and something to be treasured. Jay grew to respect how his dad moved through the forest, treating the woodland with respect.

During his time with his father, Jay found his stepmom's Bible. He looked at the margins filled with her handwriting, reading the notes she had written. He felt respect nudge him for the time she spent reading this book. On Sunday, he quietly rose and prepared to attend church. He watched the respectful attitude of the people as they listened to the minister talk about this book. What was it that separated church attendees from the men and women he met on the streets?

When he graduated from high school, many of his classmates were moving on to college. Jay had excelled in art but he was uncertain about what route to follow. Should he attend college or find a job and get his own place? A pastor suggested that he take a look at a small Bible-based college in North Dakota. The courses were not accredited but Jay thought he might further explore Christian belief. For three years he attended classes before deciding that he would transfer to a community college to get the basic credits toward an accredited degree.

Returning to Los Angeles, he enrolled in a community college. In keeping with the three years at the Bible college, he began attending Calvary Chapel, listening to the teaching of Pastor Chuck Smith. During coffee hour, he listened to the conversations that swirled around him. Many of the people seemed to boast about how they lived and what they were doing to show they were Christians. Yet, when he turned to the Bible, he saw that God called for humility and surrender. He wondered, if this pattern of behavior was what God desired, why did he not feel comfortable around the Christian community?

In the hours away from classes, he worked in construction to pay the rent on an apartment. On the job site, he began to make friends that had little desire to attend a church. He soon found he was losing interest in the church. Sundays were a day off when he could relax and do what he enjoyed. Jay struggled to align the dark thoughts and his longing for alcohol and drugs with a desire to follow the God of light and goodness.

Disillusioned, he began to move away from the church. He told God, "After all these years, I can't seem to get it together and I'm tired of being miserable. Until you show me what is true, I'm not going to pretend."

Jaybyrd

Chapter 2

Jay soon lost interest in finishing an Associate degree. He ran heavy equipment on construction sites during the week and looked for a good time on weekends. He hung out with old friends he had known from his earlier years. Weekends were for drinking, marijuana and living easy until another work week rolled around.

Soon one of his friends introduced Jay to metamphetamines which gave him a sense of euphoria and energy. He bought his first Harley and became one of the men he had so admired as a kid. He was free to rumble down the city streets as others watched him ride into the distance. If he heard any whisper of his earlier belief, if he heard God speak to him, he brushed the moment aside. Yet, there must have been some sense that he was straying into darkness and making poor choices.

The allure of heroin lies in the sense that nothing is important anymore. We can cast off our regrets and live in the moment. The moment is what is real, not some God who taps us on the shoulder and calls us to sacrifice our own desires and live in Him. The men he hung with introduced him to heroin and cocaine. The construction job lost its allure. Weekend parties started early and stretched into the work week.

As his drug use became more expensive, Jay, using a pistol, held up a restaurant. His crime spree did not last long. Within weeks, he was arrested for armed robbery and sent to prison. As he sat in the small cell, he thought back to the days when he had walked among the tall spruce and fir in the mountains of Oregon. He thought of his step-mother and her disappointment in the choices he was making. He resolved to return to the building trades when he was released. And he would return to church, he would make a new start.

Prisons have a number of programs for prisoners seeking a new life, some are approved by the prison administration, other programs are more informal and conducted by the inmates. Ultimately, time drags as the men wait out each day. They watch each other, they watch the guards. Released into the yard, a set of weights offers the prisoners a focal point as they build muscle and compare records.

Of his time spent in prison, Jay described the experience as "a training program in learning to be a better criminal." A wry smile crossed his face.

After his release, Jay found a construction firm willing to employ a convicted criminal and made an effort to go straight. For three years, he followed the trade, rising early, driving heavy equipment throughout the day. The job paid the bills.

Then, economic recession struck in the early 1980s. Construction projects were halted. The banks were unwilling to fund construction loans to all but the largest construction firms. With so few buildings going up, the number of men applying for a job doubled, tripled. The numbers of unemployed soared.

Jay found himself unemployed without a prospect for another job. He had made a living of sorts in the drug trade and now returned to selling illegal drugs. Better yet, he knew a man who was cooking speed, the slang for amphetamines.

In the 1960s, marijuana had been the drug of choice for young people flooding into southern California, seeking freedom from the expectations of older generations. Many had moved on to LSD and heroin. In time, many of those who had lived on the beaches and streets of southern California had grown disillusioned with the rhetoric of free love and drugs, choosing to return to traditional occupations and home ownership. But the wall between the illicit drug culture and traditional society had been breached. As the former flower children drove themselves to succeed, they were not above using amphetamines to give them a burst of energy. Amphetamines give the user a sense that anything is possible.

Every two weeks, Jay picked up a batch of metamphetamines and made a loop throughout southern California, selling the metamphetamines to his clientele and picking up new customers along the way. He was making money and his customers looked to him as their supplier.

One afternoon, he pulled up to a bar and strolled in, on the prowl for new clients. A pretty young lady with red hair caught his eye. Sue remembers looking up at this tall, handsome guy with broad shoulders and an infectious grin. Handsome, yes but she thought he dressed a bit preppy. He was too clean cut and straight laced for her taste. She preferred men a bit on the wild side. However, something clicked for Jay and he asked her out. While Sue like to have a good time, she was wary of men she did not know. She suggested they meet while she cared for her horse. They could talk as she groomed the animal.

The next evening, after seeing Jay, a drug dealer came over to her home, exchanging drugs for cash. She was afraid of him and pulled out a .45 caliber pistol. Sitting on the couch, she clicked the safety on and off as they talked. Jay arrived at her door and she was glad to see him as she already sensed that he would not allow the dealer to harm her. Following that encounter, she became more willing to trust him.

Today, she laughs at her first impression of him, saying his clean cut appearance and preppy clothes were his way of keeping the police from suspecting that he might be selling drugs. They began dating.

After they first met, Jay continued to sell drugs on a circuit though southern California. His courier route came to a sudden demise when he was arrested for the transportation and selling of metamphetamines. He was sentenced to a three-year term in the California Institute for Men, known in popular lore as Chino State Prison. Sue was also arrested as she was with him. Jay chose to take the bulk of the charges on himself, in an attempt to protect her.

Chino was built in 1941 as a prison without a security perimeter to house those convicted of non-violent crimes.

Jaybyrd

The prison was designed to house just under 3,000 inmates. By 2010, the population was stretching upwards of 5,000 inmates. In a large institution, the consequences go well beyond the initial sentence. The prisoners are now identified by a number with their name a secondary identifier. They are taken to a processing center where they exchange their clothing for prison garb. Every movement of their lives is choreographed either by the procedures of the institution or by the culture in the exercise yard.

Men sent to prison build an identity. Jay honed his ability to remain very stoic while observing what was happening around him. Along with using the weight-lifting equipment in the exercise yard, Jay returned to his interest in painting, further developing his skill and artistic talent.

Over his three-year term, he determined that he must make some major changes in his life as he did not want to return to prison. He now had two strikes against him in his criminal record. To combat the increase in criminal activity, California had passed a law, requiring that an offender with three felony convictions be sent to prison for 25 years.

By the very nature of the life he had chosen, Jay thought he was at risk of earning a third conviction. He thought it might be best to leave California when he was released from prison. After completing her six week term in prison, Sue had opted to move east while she waited for Jay's release.

He was twenty-six years of age upon release and would see the inside of a prison three more times before he radically chose to change the direction of his life.

Chapter 3

After his release from Chino, Jay left California. His father was now living in Bouse, a small town on the Arizona side of the border, near the Colorado River. Jay found a job flipping burgers at Al's Riverside Bar in the little town of Parker, a few miles north of Bouse. He moved in with his dad. When Sue returned to Arizona, they found a small place to live. Along with Jay, she was employed at Al's as a bartender.

The Colorado River flows south through the Sonoran Desert, a green line of vegetation carved through a sea of sand and rock. There is no major industry in Parker other than the tourism that survives on the trade along the river. Visitors come to the river to play in the cool water and catch a tan under the blazing sun. In the summer months, temperatures can reach 120 degrees. Cool river water is the antidote for the overheated temperatures. Most bars and restaurants closed by 8:00 in the evening. All of this was very different from the life that Jay had known in southern California.

Jay had never cooked a meal but what is there to throw-

Jay & Harley, roadside stop

ing a burger on the grill? Flipping burgers and bar tending, the weeks passed until the day when the police arrived. Sue watched the police enter the bar, wondering who they had come to question. The owner was not on the premises but she passed on his contact information and uneasily peered through the window as they left. Jay stood behind her, watching the police leave. They glanced at each other, each thinking of their past record, before returning to work.

Closing time rolled around and they eagerly locked the door. As they rolled back to their small home, they divided the chores between them. They had an old truck that Jay was repairing. He quickly began sliding parts into place and tightening bolts while Sue worked to gather their possessions and pack them into bags and boxes. That night, they left town with a note to their boss, saying they would no longer be working for Al's River Bar. Neither of them could imagine what the police might be seeking but they thought most likely that a charge from the past had caught up with them. They were using drugs though Sue preferred the legal high of alcohol. They imagined that it was just a matter of time till Jay was arrested again.

Arriving in Flagstaff, a town in the mountains of northern Arizona, Jay began looking around for a job. He knew the construction trade and held a commercial drivers license. Babbitts Wholesale was willing to hire a man with a felony record in their construction yard, assisting customers and making deliveries.

The Babbitt Brothers were merchants, who had arrived in Flagstaff in the early 1900s. Their enterprise included a chain of trading posts and a department store in downtown Flagstaff. A storefront sold plumbing and electrical supplies to retail shoppers while out back, the wholesale yard supplied the construction industry. Jay was earning $5 an hour, significantly less than he had made as a drug courier.

He briefly thought of his paintings done in the time at Chino. He loved painting and sketching, showing considerable artistic talent. Could he make a living as an artist?

"You have to be dead for a couple of hundred years," he said with a wry smile. As much as he might have wanted to sell his art work, he considered painting to be a hobby pursued in his spare time.

While working at Babbitts, Jay would cross the street to pick up lunch at a small deli owned by Bonnie Estes. Bonnie's father had given up farming in Colorado to move to Flagstaff. Born and raised in Flagstaff, she knew the town well.

"Jay had a great smile. He was funny and easy going. We became good friends."

Jay would hang out, chatting with Bonnie as he ate, and then return to his deliveries. Neither knew at the time how tight their friendship would become in the years that followed.

In 1989, Harley riders gathered at H & H Cycles on the eastern edge of town. Jesse Sensibar had just arrived in Flagstaff and lived in the forest a half mile from the bike shop. For those who loved Harley Davidson motorcycles and the bike culture, H & H was a good place to hang out. Jesse had arrived in town with a bag of cocaine. He quickly found a social circle. The two men, Jay and Jesse, became friends, sharing a love of motorcycles and the use of illegal drugs.

Jay and Sue rented a trailer fifteen miles east of town. Jay had a small cement out-building apart from the trailer that he used as an art studio when he wasn't working. They found a group of friends and enjoyed parties out in the high country away from town. Jesse recalls one night, returning from a party when Susan fell asleep on Jay's lap as Jesse drove them home. With each rut and pothole, her head hit the dashboard of the truck. Under the influence Jay seemed insensible to her condition. She never felt the blows as the alcohol and drugs she had consumed left her insensible.

In time, Jay asked Sue to marry him. She laughs as she recalls their honeymoon. They decided to ride to Florida on his Harley hard-tail. Sue lasted one day perched on the bike behind Jay. The term hard-tail refers to the pre-World War II bikes with little to cushion the feel of every rut and bump along the road. Those perched on the back, feel every nuance of the asphalt under the bike's tires. Harley would later add better suspension to cushion the ride.

As they rode east, pain spread across Sue's back and she had to tell Jay that she would be unable to continue behind him on the Harley. The next day, they rented a car and for the remainder of the trip, she followed him as he rode the Harley across the continent, passing through state after state.

When Arizona went through another recession, Jay lost his job at Babbitt Wholesale. He began to consider how he might use his artistic talents to earn a living. Jay liked the look of a tattoo but had no training in applying ink to skin.

*Jesse called the painting, 'Moses',
Jay titled the work, 'Shark Attack'*

"The people I hung out with, we all liked tattoos," he explained. "We just figured out how to do it."

I considered the permanence of a tattoo and what one would do with those first attempts as the artist worked to gain some experience. Tats are just so permanent!

In 1993, Jesse and a business partner opened Rata Tatoo. The small tat shop was down a flight of stairs in the basement of a local restaurant on the south side of the railroad tracks running through downtown Flagstaff. At the time, tattoo artists were very protective of their trade and their equipment. Jesse recalls that it was difficult to buy a tat gun and find a mentor who would instruct a novice in the trade. Much of the art was lined in black and filled with shades of gray. Consider the old tatoos on a sailor home on leave. This was the traditional tat.

Jesse hired Ryan Julien to work at Rata Tatoo. Julien had done his first tats in Jesse's livingroom. Jesse, for his part, wanted nothing to do with their early efforts but he began nudging Jay to unobtrusively learn what he could. Both Jay and Ryan were well built, topping out at six foot, four inches. Yet, Julian was a bit uncomfortable with Jay peering over his shoulder, learning the trade. Jay acquired a used gun and began to experiment on friends and his own skin. His skill as an artist led him to mix his colors and begin shading the images, creating tats that were very colorful compared to the black and gray of the fifties.

Clients began to find their way into the small shop at the bottom of the steps and Jay created beautifully shaded works of art across their skin. Sue would described the tats as

A portrait of David Maestas / Jaybyrd

appearing to be paintings, superior to the elemental work of many tat artists.

West Coast tattoo artists began to hear about a little shop in a town in the mountains of Arizona. One by one, they would drop in and spend a few days hanging out, creating a few tats.

Jesse mounted one of Jay's paintings behind the counter. The painting is an iconic portrayal of a bearded man on a bike carving through the surf of a California beach. Jesse called the painting *Moses* for the parting of the waves. Whether the canvas was living flesh or fabric or art board, Jay exercised his artistic skills in creating beautiful work that often portrayed a darkness in his soul.

Jesse hired David Maesta, another tattoo artist with a prison record. David pulled out a prison tat gun made from a cassette motor duck-taped together with spring steel and an ink cartridge and needle. His specialty was a tat with a fine black line outlining his work. The shop now had multiple artists, each with a specialty in the tattoo business.

In 1994, friends arranged an art show for Jay in a gallery in California. He carefully packed his paintings and shipped them to the west coast. For a man who felt he could not make a living with his paintings, the show gave him a sense of validation.

The same year, Bonnie, the friend from his truck-driving days, learned of an abandoned house out beyond Sunset Crater National Monument. At one point, a developer title the area Alpine Ranchos and sold lots to those wishing to live off the grid. This may be a bit of a misnomer as the area bears no resemblance to an a pastoral alpine setting. Living off the grid may sound appeal but for many the reality quickly becomes overwhelming. Some dragged recreational vehicles out to their lots. Others built cabins or basic structures. The allure quickly faded and some simply walked away from their investment, leaving the structures behind.

Bonnie's dad had frequently reminded her that everyone should have his own pience of dirt. "They're not making it anymore!"

When her husband described the abandoned house, she was willing to look at it.

"I didn't own any dirt," she says. They bought the property which consisted of the building and 23 acres, no electricity, no water. It became their retreat during the summer months where their children could play outdoors.

As the years slid by, Jay and Susan's marriage began to disintegrate. Susan could not understand that Jay refused to be attracted to the women who passed through the tat shop and demanded to know if Jay was faithful to her. For his part, Jay insisted that she was the only one he wanted in his life. There was no other woman.

When Jay had was arrested for driving under the influence (DUI), he served time again in one of the largest prisons in Arizona. Perryville was a common destination for those jailed on either DUI or drug charges. Unlike Chino, Perryville has different levels of units from medium security escalating to maximum security to the unit commonly called Death Row. The prison has an enclosed security perimeter.

Some of the buildings do not have air conditioning. Prisoners reside in small cells with around 85 square feet of space containing a bunk and toilet. Exercise is in chain link cages rather than an open yard. One inmate described the facility as very lonely and isolating.

When he was released in 1996, Sue was ready to move on. She had stayed with him through his time in prison but she recognized that every party comes to an end.

Sue could see the physical degradation from the drugs and alcohol but neither she nor Jay seemed to be able to break free of their drug use. She identifies the use of alcohol and drugs as self-medicating.

"Why do you think people choose to drink and get high?" I asked.

"Because they are in pain and the drugs relieve the pain of the past. The drug gives them a sense of euphoria and well-being for however long the high lasts."

She began to see the party-fueled life as a dead-end. She left Jay and moved back to her parents' home. One evening, after consuming a bottle of wine, she began to sob, dropping on her knees to the floor.

She cried out to God, "I want to go straight and I can't leave alcohol alone even for my parents or the ones I love. God help me."

Twenty-four years later, she still attends Alcoholics Anonymous meetings weekly, if not daily. She has a sponsor who stands beside her when temptation tugs at her will to leave alcohol in the past. She has rebuilt her life and counts her relationship with God as a daily walk and the key to her survival.

During the years with Sue, Jay had some contact with the outlaw motorcycle gangs but he was not interested in signing on with one of these criminal organizations. The tattoo business is part of the outlaw culture as tats identify a man and his alliance to a gang. Sue recalls that the outlaw gangs were certainly interested in Jay. They offered to patch him over without the trial basis required of most recruits. Jay refused their efforts to recruit him.

Years later, with a wry smile, Jay would recall asking a gang member "if they offered major medical and dental coverage." He never became a member of an outlaw gang.

The police had also taken notice of Jay and suspected that he was being recruited. They began to pressure him to become an informant. It seemed to Jay that either way, outlaw biker or informant, he would have a target on his back. He had no interest in risking either jail or a deadly confrontation as an informant. He began to think it might be best if he left Flagstaff.

As year 2000 rolled around, Jay and a friend packed their belongings and moved to the small town of Showlow in eastern Arizona. Showlow is in the White Mountains and much of the economy is based on government entities, ranching or the tourism industry. Jay thought the town could use its first tat shop.

Some of the residents, primarily of the establishment and those of the Latter Day Saints thought otherwise. A friend helped him find space to set up his tat shop. And he went to work inking skin while his partner was selling illegal drugs. They found their reception to Showlow could get a bit heated. As the community learned of their presence, they were threatened and told to leave town. But, others began making their way to the tat shop for a an inscription on their skin.

On June 18, 2002, a woman found herself stranded on a lonely dirt road near Showlow. As the hours passed, a surge of panic overcame her. Her companion had gone for help with their broken-down truck. She had waited hours for his return. Finally, to attract attention to her location, she set fire to a bush. The blaze was the beginning of one of Arizona's largest wild fires. The flames swept through the dry forests of the back country, using narrow canyons as chimneys to intensify the spread of the flames. Showlow lay directly in the path of this wildfire. Residents nervously watched as the column of smoke drew closer. They huddled around televisions to catch the latest report on the fire's progress, wondering if they would be called to evacuate. Others climbed on tractors to battle the flames but their efforts seemed stymied by the winds and lack of moisture. As the monsoonal rains returned around the fourth of July, rain began to fall in parts of northern Arizona.

By July 7, the firefighters made some progress and the fire began to come under containment. When the fire was declared fully contained, it had burned 468,638 acres. The flames stopped short of Showlow but for a region that relied heavily on tourism and outdoor recreation, the fire was devastating. As the number of visitors dropped, business declined in the town. Jay found the demand for his business dried up as well. No one was coming in for a tat.

He sat in the quiet shop, reviewing his life. He had been in and out of prison for the last 20 years. His partner was gone as well as his business. He was asking God to help him change but he did not know how to make the change happen.

"I was looking for a way out," he said

When you rely on a dark trade and on illegal drugs to bring food to the table, it is very hard to leave the lifestyle that is supporting you. Despite his criminal record and his use of illegal drugs, his past encounters with the Christian faith continued to drift through his thoughts. He had not forgotten his step-mother's Bible and her notes fading into the margins of each page. As he thought about his life over the years, he recognized the life he was living was dark and would lead to his destruction.

In the silence, he spoke to God.

"I am so tired of this life! I don't know how to make a change. I don't know what I should do. I can't do this in my own strength. Help me to turn around."

Then, he heard God ask, "Do you really want out?"

Jay left the tat shop and drove over to see the friend who had helped him set down roots in Showlow. He handed off everything he owned related to motorcycles, including a broken down Harley. His friend didn't want to take Jay's Harley or the shop.

"You don't want to do this, man."

"I'm getting out," Jay told his friend. "I'm moving to

Jaybyrd

Flagstaff. Look, I still owe you for setting me up with the shop and all. I'll give you the shop and I'll pay you the remainder of what I owe you when I get it."

Jay left Showlow, owing the man $500. Returning to Flagstaff, he began inking skin again at Rata Tattoo. He shaved his head and beard, changing his appearance. His friend, Jesse, had moved into a small house just north of downtown Flagstaff. With her husband in jail, Bonnie had filed for divorce. She moved into the house on Elm. Jay needed a place to live and they invited him to live on Elm as well. The three began to form a family unit.

Their friends flowed in and out of the house. To the neighbors, the traffic must have looked like a couple of guys enjoying life and friendship. But there was a darker side to life on Elm Street. Jesse had learned to cook meth, the street name for a chemical cocktail that produces a sense of euphoria and well being. Jay had been steadily using drugs since being released from prison in California.

"Jay was kind of a guru on all things speed," recalled Jesse. "I became his dealer. I kept meth in a drawer next to my bed. Jay and Bonnie dipped into my supply whenever they wanted to get high."

"How much was he using," I asked.

"He was using all the drugs he could get and I became the purveyor of all temptations. I don't know about the heroin as I didn't deal in that. I supplied the meth. He was doing about a grand a week."

"That's an expensive habit."

"Yeah. Going back to the early 1990s, we were moving

a lot of crank and cocaine. I remember one day I came home with the front page of the Arizona Daily Sun. The headline read something like, A Demon Stalks Flagstaff. The article talked about the illegal drugs that were being sold in town and we knew the article was about us even though we weren't named. We thought it was kind of cool to be called demons." He paused for a moment, reflecting. "You know, we probably deserved to be in jail or dead for some of the things we did."

Jay continued using heroin and amphetamines. Again a wry smile, as he mentioned nodding off on heroin as he was working on a tat.

"Oops, I can fix that!"

Today, you can find a number of people with tats from Jay around Flagstaff. His skill as an artist drew clients to the shop. In his spare time, he continued to spread paint over canvas, either selling or trading his work. But with his drug use, one possession after another slipped through his fingers. He lost everything that had any value.

Over several months, Jay had two accidents that would bring his life to a turning point. In moving from Showlow to Flagstaff, he rolled his Nissan truck, totaling the vehicle.

Jesse had purchased an industrial lot in west Flagstaff, intending to use the central building as an office for his towing business. Jay, having left the business where he was employed over a dispute with his employer, opened his own business in a small room in an adjoining building.

Jesse loaned Jay a truck. The man was in the towing business and vehicles filled his yard. Driving south on Interstate 17, Jay nodded off as he approached Camp Verde.

His truck veered from the roadway, tumbling into a ravine. The police, reading the registration, called Jesse and he soon arrived to find his 1972 GMC truck totaled. As it rolled, the truck struck a large tree at a point between the cab and the truck bed, cleaving the two apart. The Sergeant investigating the accident, found a baggie of heroin wrapped in an old shirt in the truck's cab.

Due to his towing business, Jesse knew the officers that patrolled this stretch of highway. After a quiet discussion, the Sergeant wrote the citation for 'misdemeanor possession of narcotics', a charge that does not exist in the Arizona Legal Code. Jay avoided another prison sentence. He was badly hurt with a head injury but refused medical attention, likely knowing the heroin in his blood would force hospital personnel to file a report.

Again, within just a few months, another incident occurred though not so serious. Jay was driving a 1962 Chevy truck, again borrowed from Jesse. He had loaded cans of paint, brushes, canvas and other supplies in the truck bed. Driving east along Interstate 40, past Winslow toward Holbrook, he glanced in his rear view mirror to see flames rising out of the supplies in the back of the truck. Taking a moment to consider his options, he knew that if he stopped, the flames would consume the supplies. He had no fire extinguisher. If he kept going, the wind would fan the flames, accelerating the rate of burn. No good options, he kept driving. I suspect that he thought he might reach a location where he could extinguish the flames.

Other motorists had noticed the flames in the bed of the truck and called the Highway Patrol. An officer caught up to Jay, pulled alongside and motioned Jay to follow them. They escorted the truck to the Love's Truck Stop in Joseph City, between Holbrook and Winslow. Having notified the fire department, a fire truck was waiting to extinguish the fire. Despite the damage, the truck was still driveable and Jesse continued to use the vehicle, crinkled paint and all, after the incident.

As 2003 came to an end, Jay was 50 years of age. He knew he needed to transform his life but he couldn't seem to make the needed changes. He says he was so immersed in a lifestyle of drugs and ink that he seemed unable to find a way out. He knew he didn't want to become a member of any church but he wanted to learn more of God.

He began to ask, "What is real? How am I to live?"
Then, God spoke again.
"Time to begin."

First of all, faith is not an emotion, not a feeling. It is not a blind subconscious urge toward something vaguely supernatural. It is not simply an elemental need in man's spirit. It is not a feeling God exists.

But also it is not an opinion. It is not a conviction based on rational analysis. It is not the fruit of scientific evidence.

Faith is first of all an intellectual ascent. It perfects the mind, it does not destroy it. It puts the intellect in possession of Truth which reason cannot grasp by itself.

~ Thomas Merton

New Seeds of Contemplation, Thomas Merton, New Directions Publishing Company, 1962, page 126-127 (passage condensed).

Part Two

Chapter 4

Allison Israel came out of the Jewish conclaves of New York City. She moved to Flagstaff to earn a degree in archeology. One evening, two friends invited her along on a visit to a local tattoo parlor. They each intended to get a tat and teased her a little about what she might have inked onto her skin.

Allison was not about to get a tatoo. She needed to think about this a long while. As Jay worked the ink under the skin, she watched him. The man did not smile. He didn't say much, a grim aura seem to surround him. But one needs to be open minded and she worked to accept Jay for the image he presented.

Years passed and Allison decided that she would indeed get her first tat. She remembered Jaybyrd at Rata Tatoo and dropped down the stairs below street level to the tattoo shop. The man she had first met was still inking skin.

As he worked, she reminded him that she had once come to the shop and watched as he inked art onto her friends. He began to talk about the years that had passed. And he talked about the love of God. A bit startled, Allison looked at him and realized that the tears were rolling down his face.

"He was weeping as he talked to me about how much God loved him!" she recalled. "There was such a difference between the man I had met years earlier and the man who was now working on me. Same man, big difference. He was crying over the love of God!"

This really hit her. She had grown up in the presence of the Jewish Torah and all the traditions of those who follow the Orthodox traditions. But she had never seen a man who wept over the love that God held for one individual. She began to ask how this transformation had occurred. He was smiling, talking, seemingly happy. He seemed to be transformed.

Today, Allison would plant the roots of this transition in the grace and forgiveness of the Almighty God, the creator of all we know. She came to believe that the God she had known as a child, had come to earth, taking the form of a man. This man had sacrificed his life and then, in a supernatural act risen back to life with the power to forgive mankind for the evil deeds we commit. Jay helped Allison to understand that what he believed could be her belief as well. She made the decision to follow Jesus, the one she calls her Messiah, her redeemer.

In time, she met a young man named Lance, they married and Jay spent considerable time with them in their home in Washington. Allison was one of the first people to witness the transformation that came over Jay when he made the decision to begin walking with God.

David Menne was the owner of the Franklin Gallery, located next door to the house on Elm Street. When Jay moved in next door, he would wander over to spend thirty minutes, sometimes an hour, talking with David. Creativity and art were their common ground. They soon found more in common.

"What did you talk about," I asked.

"We talked mostly about spiritual topics. I asked a lot of questions and Jay did most of the talking. He told me of his desire to live out in the woods away from all the distractions in life."

"So what was he thinking about his life at that point?"

"I remember he seemed filled with gratitude for what God had done for him. He began talking a lot about his desire to moved out into the forest and live alone. He seemed to think he could enter a deeper relationship with God if he could move away from all the distractions."

When a person steeped in bad choices suddenly falls on his knees out of desperation and turns to God, the difference in his or her life can be dramatic. For others, the process is a slow turning toward faith over months, even years. David remembers that Jay simply began to trust God, to believe that the God of the Bible was sovereign. He began to read, to talk more avidly with the creator and, in turn, this flowed outward to touch those who came within his influence.

Jay's friendships with women were unusual. Women may love their boyfriends and husbands but they don't always feel accepted by these men. The women I interviewed talked about how Jay accepted them for who they were without judging them.

Like Bonnie, many of the women counted Jay as a

friend who cared about them and wanted the best for them. If he suspected harm might come to them, he quietly worked to intervene.

Bonnie remembers telling Jay some of her darkest thoughts. He listened and responded with a simple, "okay." That was all, no condemnation. Jay knew he had come from a very dark place and now lived under God's grace. Bonnie credits Jay with helping her understand what her husband was experiencing in jail before their divorce and to see that his influence was leading her down a dark path.

As I've interviewed some of the women who knew Jay, I am struck by his kindness to them. After a serious stroke, one friend, Dawn had been confined to a wheelchair for a period of time. Jay frequently visited Dawn, taking the time to eat lunch with her as they talked about their lives and their common faith.

Again, Bonnie recalls that she had been a heavy drug user, along with Jay, for eight years. He was working to get clean after his return from Showlow. Then, Jesse gave up the drug trade and his personal drug use. The two of them came to Bonnie with an ultimatim.

"They told me I had two options. I could either get clean or I could find someplace else to live. These guys were my best friends and they gave a shit about me. They told me they would support me in the struggle to get clean."

As the drugs began to leave her body, Bonnie sought refuge in sleep. The drugs had been her medication for dealing with the pain and trauma that she had experienced in life. Without the drugs, she had to face her grief without the chemically-induced high. Sleeping allowed her to avoid facing the pain of withdrawal as well as the pain of the past.

On a particularly bad day, she lay in bed, her body wracked with pain, her mind equally grim. She heard the door to her bedroom open. She watched Jay place a baggie of marijuana on her dresser.

"What the fuck am I to do with that?" she snarled. The door silently closed and she lay there, angry and uncomfortable. An hour later, the door opened again. Jay quietly placed a baggie on the dresser. After he left, curious, she rose to see what he had left for her. The baggie contained hold-rolled joints of marijuana she could smoke to soften the pain of withdrawal. She nearly wept for the compassion Jay had shown toward her as she snarled at him. She lit her first joint and settled back into the pillows.

Unlike Jay, she described Jesse as high energy with a big personality. Bonnie describes herself as sometimes a bit strung out from the trauma of her past and the challenges of life. Living with the two of them, Jay was the quiet center around which they revolved.

"I think Jay became the big brother that Jesse never had," she added. The three friends had a very special relationship.

Yet, despite his kindness toward his friends, she remembers that after Jay returned to Flagstaff he seemed to be floundering.

Jay remembers thinking that as a 20-year old kid, he "didn't know nothing." In 2003, with a lifetime of experience, he was no longer satisfied with his life. He began to think about the pain he had inflicted on others and the mental pain he lived with day after day. Like many, he read Buddhist philosophy and found elements of truth in Buddhism. From his reading, he explained that our suffering is born out of our desires. And Jay certainly experienced this. However, he found no sense of completion in Buddhism.

He began asking God what needed to change. He didn't want to become a Catholic or a Baptist or join some church but how else could he pursue the God of the Bible? Millions of people across the world follow the Christian faith but almost no one today chooses to give away their possessions and takes up residence in a hovel in a wilderness. Where did Jay come up with this idea of moving out into the wilderness? Why did he feel the need to move into isolation?

For months, Jay talked about his desire to live in the wilderness where he might be alone with God, one-on-one. No distractions.

At first, he talked about going out for 40 days. In the Biblical account, four different men were taken into the wilderness to spend time with God. Moses, a Jewish man raised by Pharoah's daughter, had fled into the wilderness of Midian after murdering another Egyptian. Elijah, a prophet of Israel, had fled from an angry queen after he slaughtered her pagan priests. The Apostle Paul, the author of many New Testament books, was sent into the wilderness, escaping his angry brethren as he prepared for a ministry that would shake the Roman Empire to its roots. Jay saw these men as desirable examples as he began to walk with God. He also discovered modern examples of men, like Thomas Merton,

Some men have perhaps become hermits with the thought that sanctity could only be attained by escape from other men But the only justification for a life of deliberate solitude is the conviction that it will help you to love not only God but also other men. If you go into the desert merely to get away from people you dislike, you will find neither peace nor solitude; you will only isolate yourself with a tribe of devils.

Man seeks unity because he is the image of the One God. Unity implies solitude, and hence the need to be physcially alone. But unity and solitude are not metaphyscial isolation. He who isolates himself in order to enjoy a kind of interdependence in his egotistic and external self does not find unity a all, for he disintegrates into a muliplicity of conflicting passions and finally end in confusion and total unreality. Solitude is not and can never be a narcissistic dialogue of the ego with itself. Such self-contemplation is a futile attempt to establish the finite self as infinite, to make it permanently independent of all other beings. And this is madness. ~ Thomas Merton

New Seeds of Contemplation, Thomas Merton, New Direc tions Publishing Company, 1962, page 52 who chose to pursue solitude to pursue a deeper spiritual life.

He read that Jesus had lived in the wilderness for forty days and decided to adopt this as his example. He would step away from the distractions for 40 days in his quest to listen to God. He would take his Bible and other reading material with camping equipment and supplies. Years earlier he had learned much of living outdoors with his father on their camping trips. He was not a complete novice.

Even as he thought about the preparation required, he wasn't quite sure how to step out of the daily grind. He was living in a home where others were not committed to a walk of faith. Illegal drugs were easily available and he continued to use heroin and meth. Friends frequently dropped by. Jay began to see the friends and drugs as a distraction to the life he wished to pursue.

Jesse watched this transformation. He listened to Jay's ideas about moving out to the wilderness. He was becoming concerned about Jay's heavy drug use and the long term consequences. He didn't want to see him become a strung-out, brain-fried druggie. Maybe, as Jay's supplier, a sense of responsibility had begun to creep over him. Living with your supplier made it too easy to reach an altered state. Jesse began to think that an abrupt break from the culture they lived in might be necessary if Jay was to break free from the drugs.

In February 2004, Jay was fired from his job. Period. You're done. Out of here!

He felt as if he had been cut loose to act on the desire he had been expressing for months. He loaded a duffle bag, with an old-fashion sleeping bag lined with flannel. The bag was heavy, not an ultra light bag stuffed into a 12 by 6 inch roll.

The next item was a tent. Shaking his head, Jay said it was a really crappy tent. He added food and supplies, a pair of snowshoes and a Bible. And books. He had a map and a compass. He knew nothing about the Sycamore Wilderness.

A friend loaded the duffle into his jeep with 4-wheel-drive. They drove south out of Flagstaff toward the rim of Sycamore Canyon. Flagstaff sits in the middle of one of the largest yellow pine forests in the world. The road south crossed miles of forested terrain, the rutted dirt surface rattling the shocks of any vehicle.

In February 2004, Flagstaff still received around 120 inches of snow a year. Often, February would have a brief window of warm weather before the storms of March rolled in. In the back country, the snow would lie a foot or more in depth.

They drove within five miles of the rim of Sycamore Canyon. The road was blocked by heavy drifts of snow they could not cross, even with 4-wheel-drive. Jay's friend pulled to a stop and sat looking at the drift before them.

"I don't know, Byrd. I don't feel good about leaving you out here."

Jay grinned and opened the door, dropping his leg out of the Jeep to stand in a foot of snow. He turned and pulled the duffle from the Jeep. Stretching his arms, he looked up at sky and sucked in a deep breath of air. His smile lit his face.

The road lay ahead, covered in snow, as a lane between the ponderosa pine. After the Jeep disappeared, Jay began to snowshoe down the lane, dragging his duffle. Even if he lost the road, he could follow his compass south as Sycamore Canyon stretches across the horizon, a barrier to road traffic.

The first day, he walked nearly three miles, pulling the duffle. Walking on snowshoes, even with long legs, is tiring as the gait is unnatural. He made camp and heated a can of soup as darkness settled in. He tried to raise the tent but as noted earlier, the tent, in his words, was really crappy. He settled for sleeping under the stars, staring upward as slumber stole over him.

He woke as the first rays of sunlight lightened the branches overhead. Only silence reached his ears. No traffic, no voices, no sirens or television. Just silence. A raven lighted on a branch overhead and expressed his curiosity about this person laying on the ground below.

Wra-ack, wra-ack!

Jay lay there and listened to the bird. Ravens have a number of sounds they employ throughout the day. They would be the ones to drop in for a visit, rather than the human traffic that once interrupted his days. The birds are experienced marauders and will raid unattended packs, tearing open packages of food. From this point on, Jay would no longer be concerned about street crime but instead forest raiders.

He felt as if he had stepped through a threshold, into another world, devoid of all the wanting and corruption he had known. He had been released from a prison of his own design. He crawled from his sleeping bag as the sun's rays stretched across the snow around him. The brilliance of reflected light was nearly blinding. He felt as if a heavy weight had fallen from his shoulders as he stood in the silence. He packed his gear and set off, following the compass south toward the rim of the canyon.

Early in the afternoon, a sound other than bird calls broke the silence. He seemed to hear someone chopping wood. What? Had he come all this way to find a person cutting his winter wood supply? And what of the access to this region? The road along the rim canyon was blocked by drifts. As he dragged the duffle, he continued to glance around, looking for evidence of another person. A man appeared, walking through the forest, with a dog running from side to side as they moved forward.

"Hey, what are you doing here?" the man called as he approached.

"I heard the sound of you chopping wood. I guess it was you," replied Jay. "I'm out here to camp for a few days."

"I followed your track," said the man. "Jeez, it looks like you are dragging a body!"

Jay looked down at his duffle and laughed. "No, just my gear. A friend drove me as far as he could and I started walking."

As Jay talked, the man's dog moved toward Jay, his head down, nose quivering. Jay stretched out his hand toward the dog in greeting.

"My dog doesn't like people. He won't get near you."

The dog's head came up. His mouth opened in a dog's smile and he began to trot forward, jumping here and there. As Jay stepped forward, the dog ran circles around him, begging him to play.

"Well, I'll be dammed," the man said. "He doesn't like most people."

The dog ran up and began licking Jay's hand. Jay ran his hand over the dog's head and along his back. The dog jumped back, ready to race around in circles, trying to convince Jay to run after him. As they talked about the area, Jay explained that he intended to hike to the bottom of Sycamore Canyon and camp for several weeks.

The man explained that he had been living in the canyon for a couple of years and his camp was about a mile from the trail head. He invited Jay back to his camp. The two walked to the trail head and began dropping along a steep trail until they reach Kelsey spring.

Sycamore is a steep canyon designated as wilderness with many nooks and crannies seldom explored. The headwaters of the canyon lie just south of the little town of Williams and are funneled over Sycamore Falls, an intermittent waterfall that appears during the early months of the year. The course of the canyon slices through the Mogollon Rim to the scarified grasslands of the Verde Valley. In the upper region of the drainage, a shelf has formed a couple hundred feet below the rim, following the contours of the canyon. The shelf seems to have been shoved upward and then the subterranean force took a step back, resting a spell before making a final lunge upward. The rim is lined with with granite boulders, emerging among ponderosa pine and gambel oak. Both Kelsey and Dorsey springs rise along this shelf, the water coming from the high country snows that sink into the rock

Kelsey Spring

layers. The elevation of the trail head is just over 7,000 feet.

The trail to Kelsey Spring drops steeply, twisting around huge boulders. Any hiker would ponder this descent, knowing he must return along the steep incline to the rim. Visiting the site in 2020, I found the spring had been channeled into a metal tank brimming with water, located in a meadow dense in knee-high grass. Soft mud marked the channel as it flowed into the canyon. The site remains popular with visitors. As beautiful as the meadow might be, the spring is of questionable quality. Beyond Kelsey Spring, the trail follows a small drainage, one of many that dissect the canyon walls.

The two men dropped lower into the canyon, another half mile to Babe's Hole. Turning away from the spring, the man led Jay toward his camp, about a half mile further. Jay was astonished to find a camp with a shelter built from logs covered by a tarp. Nearby a platform of rock stood with a space enclosed for coals to create an outdoor oven. A fire pit provided warmth and a fire for cooking. Firewood was stacked, food supplies cached. The site was located on a slight incline, allowing rain and snowfall to drain away from the shelter. Tall pines provided shade during the warm afternoons.

Over the next couple of days, Jay learned his host was ill with cancer. He had planned to leave the camp in a couple of weeks to live in Cottonwood, intending to write a book about his life as a hermit. He offered to leave the camp to Jay.

Jay looked around, considering all that had been done. The site stood ready for him to move in. He chose to believe this was God's confirmation that he had chosen the correct course. Over the next week, the man showed Jay his routine and the skills he used to live in the wilderness. Much of this brought back memories of his dad's respect for the forest and his desire to care for his environment.

As the week came to a close, Jay decided to hike down to the floor of the canyon and follow the streambed to Parson Spring. Four miles beyond the spring the trail leaves

The great joy of the solitary life is not found simply in quiet in the beauty and peace of nature or in the song of birds or even in the peace of one's own heart. It resides in the awakening and the attuning of the utmost of the inmost heart to the voice of God - to the inexplicable, quiet definite inner certitude of one's call to obey Him, to hear Him, to worship Him here, now, today in silence and alone.

This listening and this obedience makes one's existence fruitful and give fruitfulness to all one's other acts. It is the purification and reason of one's own heart that has been long dead in sin. This is not simply a question of existing alone, but of doing with joy and understanding "the work of the cell," which is done in silence, not according to one's own choice or to the pressure of necessity, but in obedience to God, that is to say, in obedience to the simple conditions imposed by what is here and how.

The voice of God is not clearly heard at every moment; and part of the "work of the cell" is attention, so that one may not miss the sound of that voice. What this means, therefore, is not only attention to inner grace but to external reality and to one's self as a completely integrated part of that reality. Hence, this implies also a forgetfulness of oneself as totally apart from outer objects, standing in the stream of natural and human and cultural life of the moment. When we understand how little we listen, how stubborn and gross our hearts are, we realized how important this work is, and we see how badly prepared we are to do it.

~ Thomas Merton

A Vow of Conversation, Journals 1964-1965, New York: Farrar, Straus, Giroux, 1988 page 188-189 the creek behind, ascending to the rim of the canyon in the Verde Valley. He spent some time in Cottonwood and when he returned the hermit was gone. Jay settled in as the snow melted and grass began to emerge. Spring turned into summer, the forty days he had first intended stretched into months. As he reached the end of August, he made one of his trips into Flagstaff to purchase more supplies.

He learned that there was an active warrant out for his arrest on a charge of leaving California while on probation. The probation had followed his last term in jail on charges of driving under the influence and for possession of heroin. He chose to voluntarily surrender to law enforcement with the intention of clearing his record.

When he returned to the canyon, he found that the camp had been removed. He speculated that the hermit had returned, found him gone for an extended period and chose to remove the camp. Jay intended to continue living in the canyon, pursuing his desire to know God. After giving his location considerable thought, he chose to relocate the camp to a more secluded location.

Today, as home prices in Flagstaff soar beyond the means of a family with a low income, some residents choose to move into the woods. A few have tents but most live in older trailers. They have a vehicle to commute into Flagstaff for work. Jay had neither a hard-sided shelter or transportation.

He rebuilt the shelter and fireplace. The shelter was built of upright poles supporting several tarps and an old tent. He added a small fire pit inside his shelter, well vented

Babe's Hole

to provide a little warmth in the cool evenings. He showed me a video of the shelter. To one side, within the tent was his bed. Toward the center of the shelter, stood a seat near a crude bookshelf, both made of wood he scavenged from construction sites. A small platform gave him a place to work. Clothing hung from a line in another corner. The door to the shelter was in part clear plastic to allow light to enter the shelter. Rain or shine, the fireplace and fire pit were his only means of cooking. The small fire pit inside the shelter did little to warm the interior space. I asked about the temperature in the shelter in the depth of winter.

"Ten degrees above the temperature outside." He replied so crisply, I had little doubt that the winter months had been very difficult. His body would have adjusted somewhat in the cooler months but when the temperature dropped to below zero, there was no denying that his shelter was bitterly cold!

Jay would have been chopping wood daily. The ready supply of down and dead trees around his camp would have disappeared, meaning that he would have to range ever further to obtain firewood. He may have even cut down small trees, allowing them to age before chopping them into useful lengths.

Jay lived by the cycle of night and day. He would have gone to bed fairly early in the evenings as darkness moved in. In the darkness he listened as trees surrendered to gravity, as mountain lions screamed and coyotes chattered. Sometimes, he carried on a conversation with these vocal canines. One night he slept in the middle of an elk herd bedded down around his camp.

Less welcomed were the bears that visited his camp. One found a package of macaroons dampened by the summer rains. The bear left with the jar of peanut butter instead.

To provide water in his camp, he had three large containers and several smaller bottles. Two of the larger containers were collapsible. His location, a half mile from the spring known as Babe's Hole, was close enough to provide water but isolated enough to escape casual detection.

The spring emerges along a watercourse. The outlet is protected by loosely stacked rock that casually appears to be a well. On closer inspection visitors realize the water is welling up from a fracture in the rock to flow along a channel into the drainage. This spring is very important to the wildlife who come to drink in the quiet hours of the day. The site is shaded by a grove of ponderosa and black walnut trees.

Jay would lower his container into the pool, allowing the water to seep over the edge. The containers would expand as first one filled, then the other. He would place one container in his pack and wrap his arms around the other as he walked back to his camp. He was careful to step on rocks and downed logs, intent on leaving no tracks that someone might follow to his camp.

We think of water as seeming to have little weight as it flows over our hands into the sink. But, fill a bucket and try to carry it a half mile. Within yards, our fingers and arms ache as our muscles beg to be relieved of the weight.

I've found that in modern living, we are not aware of how many gallons of water we consume throughout each day. The average person is required to drink four to six cups a day. Jay, living outdoors, would have required a minimum of six to eight cups per day, depending on his activities and the temperature. Now, consider the amount of water we use for hygiene. An average eight-minute shower consumes around 17 gallons. Even a five gallon shower from a bag suspended in a tree would have required multiple trips to the spring, leaving Jay to clean up with a bucket and washcloth.

What of his food supplies? Hunting is by permit within specified time periods in Arizona. However, game is not abundant, even for a man living quietly in the forest. Raising a garden was just not feasible in the deep, narrow canyon without a perennial water source close by.

About every two weeks, Jay would climb to the canyon

rim and follow a succession of dirt roads over twenty miles to Interstate 40. At the east-bound ramp, he would stick out his thumb and wait for a ride. If he was lucky, he might catch a ride from a forest visitor long before he reached the interstate. If he couldn't catch a ride, he walked into town with the trip usually taking two days.

Jesse kept a bedroom open for Jay and he would crash for a few days. In town, he needed a couple of days to adjust to the noise and the pace of the people around him. He relished standing under a warm shower. He would ink a few tattoos to earn some cash for supplies and books. He applied for food stamps and this helped extend the cash for more books. After a couple of days, a friend would drive him back out to the trail head. Jay would unload his supplies, making multiple trips up and down the canyon walls.

The first two years, Jay chose to spend the coldest winter months in town. As the snows melted, the yearning to return to the forest would begin to build until he loaded his pack and found someone who would give him a ride out to the rim of Sycamore Canyon.

The term hermit has often been applied to those who choose to step aside from society and live alone. Turning to the dictionary, we read: *a hermit is a person who lives along in a lonely or secluded spot, often from religious motives; a recluse.*

Urban legends often describe hermits as odd or ill-tempered. We may think hermits do not like being around people. Jay was quick to deny that he was anti-social. If anything, he enjoyed being around friends.

At first, he worked to understand the transition he was

In order to know and love God as He is, we must have God dwelling in us in a new way, not only in His creative power but in His mercy, not only in His greatness but in His littleness, by which He empties Himself and comes down to us to be empty in our emptiness, and so fill us in His fullness. God bridges the infinite distances between Himself and the spirits created to love Him, by supernatural missions of His own life. The Father, dwelling in the depths of all things and in my own depths, communicates to me His Word and His Spirit. Receivng them I am drawn into His own life and know God in His own Love, being one with Him in His own Son.

~ Thomas Merton

New Seeds of Contemplation, Thomas Merton, New Direc tions Publishing Company, 1962, page 40-41 making in choosing to pursue God rather than living according to his own desires. When a man chooses to pursue God, he begins to consider what a being other than himself wants or wishes to happens. His life begins to change as he no longer lives solely for himself. The Bible compares the relationship between the believers and God to marriage between a man and a woman. With a solid marriage, this can be a good analogy. The man and the woman each choose to think of the other, taking the other into account as they move through the day and plan into the future.

When Jay was using heroin and metamphetamines, he was thinking only of himself. In the forest, the drugs were no longer available. He had given away or lost all his possessions. He was stripped of all but the most basic requirements for life with the exception of books.

He bought more books and he read!

When Martin Luther first pounded his thesis to the door of the church in Wittenburg, Germany, he challenged the heretical doctrine and traditions of the Catholic Church. This would overturn heresy practiced by the Catholic Church for centuries. One of his challenges centered on a verse found in Romans.

Luther asked: why was the church selling indulgences as a way to mitigate our sinfulness if our salvation was based on the shedding of Jesus' blood and the gift of God's grace?

This argument was based on a verse from the book of Ephesians in the New Testament:

"It is by grace we are saved, through faith and this not of

ourselves. It is the gift of God, so that no man can boast."
Ephesians 2:8

This verse would come to epitomize the freedom that Jay was seeking in exploring the Christian faith. Non-believers would ask: "Saved from what?"

When he first moved out to Sycamore, Jay mostly read the Bible, working to understand the concepts explained throughout scripture. He understood that he had broken the law of our land which is based on the laws that God gave the ancient tribes of Israel. In the past he had told God that he could not pretend to be a Christ follower anymore.

As Jesse stated earlier, by all rights, they should had both been sentenced to a lengthy term in jail or been killed for the things they had done. They were guilty under the law of the land. In God's eyes, there was nothing they could offer to satisfy a righteous God. Yet, the Bible proclaimed that his relationship with God was not based on Jay's actions. Rather, Jesus had paid the penalty for all the wrong that Jay had committed and now through God's grace, Jay had been forgiven.

I watched his hands fondle the New Testament as he marveled over God's grace in offering us salvation from our punishment for our sin, based on the sacrifice of Jesus on our behalf. After all these years he understood there was nothing he could offer that would be deemed acceptable by a holy God. Instead, God found a way to bring us to himself.

He imitated the noise of rockets exploding and exclaimed, "This just blows my mind!"

Scrounge Sculpture / Jaybyrd

Chapter 5

As I consider Jaybyrd's solitary life among the pines of northern Arizona, I looked at some of the other terms used for people who separate from society.

Recluse: a person who lives a solitary life and tends to avoid other people.

Eremite: a Christian hermit or recluse.

Anchorite: someone who, for religious reasons, withdraws from secular society so as to be able to lead an intensely prayer-oriented life.

Mystic: a person who seeks by contemplation and self-surrender to obtain unity with or absorption into the Deity or the absolute, or who seeks in the spiritual apprehension of truths that are beyond the intellect.

Actually, an anchorite was far more extreme than the average recluse. In the Middle Ages, anchorites often chose to be permanently sealed into small dwellings with food and waste passed through a small window. I shudder at such an extreme choice.

Jay had chosen to live in the forest in his pursuit of God and yet, he freely came and went as he needed supplies. He certainly wasn't a recluse. Jay was a man who seemed filled with gratitude and he shared his thankfulness with others.

By contrast, I read the story of another man who simply parked his car one day and walked into the woods. He lived by stealing from nearby cabins, surviving for a couple of decades before he was discovered breaking into a cabin. There were no spiritual implications to his pursuit of living alone. This man simply applied himself to the matter of living without any redeeming value. He did not want to be around other people. As a hermit, he simply existed.

Jay was not a recluse to the exclusion of all other concerns. He cared deeply about his friends and enjoyed their company. In fact, he thought he enjoyed their company a bit too much for his quest in life. Out of his desire to know God, he turned his intent to pursuing solitude. One could say he was a quotidian or common man's mystic. A quotidian mystic is one who pursues the mystery of God while involved in everyday activities.

Jay chose to live apart from society in order to avoid the commerce that distracted him from thinking and reading about God. Living with Jesse and working in the tattoo industry, he found the temptation to slide back into heroin use and other destructive lures enticing. Friends might stop by, drawing him away from the time he wished to spend reading and in meditation. The only way he was going to remain on this new course was to step away from the daily enticements that crossed his doorstep.

Thinking back to his early years, he had witnessed his stepmother's devotion to the all-mighty, all-present, all-knowing God. If this God was the creator of the universe as the Bible said, then this demanded something more than a day-to-day scramble for a few bucks. If this spirit had taken the form of a man, enclosing the all-mighty into human form, well, Jay's mind could not begin to comprehend this. He needed time and space to consider these ideas.

He had become curious about the men who chose to live a secluded life totally focused on God; men like the Desert Fathers who lived in isolation in the wilderness. In the second and third centuries after the resurrection of Jesus, men began to move out to the Egyptian desert west of the Nile River to live as hermits near desert wadis. The wadis are shallow depressions that retain water and draw both birds and wildlife to their shores. The perennial supply of fowl and water sustained the hermits and they built shacks along the shores as shelter while they meditated on God and the scriptures. Their expressed purpose was to remove themselves from society's distractions to concentrate on sacred and existential beliefs. Most of these men were following some form of Christian teaching.

In time, so many men moved out to the wadis that a whole society formed and cities rose out of the sands. A number of men established themselves in leadership, often taking the role of counselor or teacher. People seeking counsel made their way to these ascetics, seeking advice for

Thomas Merton / Jaybyrd

their estrangement in life. The teaching of several of these men has been preserved through the centuries. Jay found several of their literary works to consider. He respected their choice to abstain from physical comfort in a pursuit of deeper faith. This drew him to consider the idea of living in the wilderness, alone.

He also found two biographies, one was *The Seven Storey Mountain* by Thomas Merton; the other *Confessions* by Augustine, an Egyptian monk and the first archbishop of Cairo. Ironically, both men had lived a life of dissipation, squandering their early years in pursuing whatever carnal desire gratified them. Like King Solomon of the Old Testament, Augustine would eventually conclude that the physical pleasures he had pursued were of no worth. As he despaired, he heard a small child singing a rhyme that repeated the phrase, 'Take up and read.' Glancing around, Augustine discovered a copy of the Bible's New Testament. As he read, he concluded that 'only God could truly satisfy his longings.'

Merton for his part concluded that monastic life was

not sufficient for his desire to pursue godly contemplation. He appealed to the Vatican for permission to live alone in a life devoted to study, prayer and meditation. He eventually did receive permission to live alone in a Hermitage. In time he became quite taken with Buddhist monasticism.

In an earlier time, Jay had said he just could not pretend to be a Christian. He would pursue his own passions until God showed him otherwise. God had allowed him free reign to pursue whatever he wished and Jay had come to realize just how shallow pursuing pleasure can become. He wanted something of intrinsic value that would not fade as time passed.

Writer Phillip Yancy suggests that we make a god out of physical pleasure, out of sexual satisfaction or material possessions in an attempt to satisfy the desire that has been placed within us for the presence of God. He echos the phrase from Augustine, "Our hearts, oh Lord, are restless until we find our rest in thee."

As Jay studied the lives of these men, he began to recognize that he had been an unbridled spirit, doing as he pleased. He had not practiced either intellectual or spiritual discipline. For the first time Jay understood that he could discipline his mind. He could sort through and organize the thoughts that ricocheted through his mind. He was not at the mercy of whatever erupted in his head throughout the day.

This recognition encouraged him to read more books that further educated and challenged him. I've bought several of the books he recommended and they are not for the timid with small cramped type, archaic phrasing, drag-on sentences and obscure theology. Jay persevered, thinking for long hours on the ideas he read.

In one short video, Margo McClellan records Jay as saying that he was not interested in joining a self improvement group or church.

"I've been to those groups. I've been to church. I don't need that kind of thing," he insisted.

Then why did he come to church now and then? Many would applaud his sentiment but I began to understand that he was delving into a relationship with the creator of the universe that stretched far beyond whatever teaching he might gain from a short burst of doctrine from the pulpit.

He was learning discipline.

Part of becoming disciplined is the concept of self denial. In American society, we are raised to believe that we should work hard in order to acquire a home, a nice car, good food and sharp clothes. The hermit chooses to venture in quite the opposite direction. Material possessions may distract him from what is intrinsically valuable in life. Consequently, he gives away or sheds the trappings of modern life.

By choosing to live in the woods, Jay rejected a comfortable life. As noted earlier, he lived in a tent where the temperature might drop into the teens with only a small fire to keep the killing temperatures at bay.

This self-sacrifice is based on scriptures like the instructions Jesus gave to a rich young man, *"One thing you lack: Go! Sell everything you have and give to the poor, and you will have treasure in heaven. Then come, follow me."* *

Or Peter's cry, "We have left all we have to follow you."

Jesus replies, *"I tell you the truth, no one who has left home or wife or brothers or parents or children for the sake of the kingdom of God will fail to receive many times as much in this age and in the age to come, eternal life."* **

The concept of sacrifice went beyond giving up comfort to sharing in the suffering that Jesus experienced while on this earth.

Quoting Philippians 3:8-9 of the New Testament:

"But whatever was to my profit I now consider loss for the sake of Christ. What is more, I consider everything a loss compared to the surpassing greatness of knowing Christ Jesus my Lord, for whose sake I have lost all things. I consider them rubbish, that I may gain Christ and be found in him, not having a righteousness of my own that comes from a law, but that which is through faith in Christ."

Those familiar with the old teachings of the Catholic Church might fear that the idea of self denial might include small hand-held whips and raw flesh across the back. Or maybe a hair shirt worn day and night so that comfort cannot entice us away from contemplation of Jesus' sacrifice.

Jay was not adverse to comfort but he recognized that in accepting suffering, he was pursuing a greater good. He was pursuing a knowledge of God and sharing in the suffering that Christ endured on our behalf.

For those who choose to live alone, when the time

---

* Mark 10:20-21
** Luke 18:28-30

comes to return to modern life, the traffic and noise, the hustle and concern of everyday life seems alien. To those who knew the person before he took up an isolated existence, the person who returns is different. This sense of alienation is not all that different from one returning from another country after decades abroad.

The ascetic begins talking about an existence in the spirit that one cannot see with human eyes while the rest of society lives in a world where the five senses define what is real. The spirit world and the physical world are equally present but only one is easily experienced.

When Jay returned to civilization and began talking about what he was reading and learning, most of his friends failed to understand the illumination of the unseen spirit world while Jay felt the culture shift into a souless, loud maelstrom of drifting, oblivious souls.

Back with friends, he joined conversations, laughing and talking, even as he felt stymied in explaining the mystic heights he explored. He called it a time of deep introspection and reconstruction. He began to long for a mentor.

One of the fruits of the solitary life is a sense of the absolute importance of obeying God, a sense of the need to obey and to seek not as a a last resort, but as one's daily supersubstantial bread. This mean liberation from automatic obedience into the seriousness and gravity of a free choice to submit; but it is not always easy to see where and how.*

~ Thomas Merton

---

* A Vow of Conversation, Journals 1964-1965, New York: Farrar, Straus, Giroux, 1988 page 171

Scrounge Sculpture / Jaybyrd

Chapter 6

Jay did not spend all his time reading and thinking about the topics he explored. He frequently walked the trails through Sycamore Canyon. One trail near his camp led down to the floor of the canyon. Another trail followed a shelf from Kelsey Spring west to Dorsey Spring. Along these routes, Jay frequently met other hikers exploring the canyon but none found his small camp.

On at least one occasion, he followed the stream through Sycamore Canyon down to Parson Spring and beyond to the town of Cottonwood.

As Jay finished out his fifth year in the canyon, he may have been unaware that he was not the only man living in the depths of Sycamore. A young couple chose a day to hike down to Dorsey Spring with the option of exploring beyond. By the time they reached Dorsey Spring, the young woman had become a bit weary and was reluctant to proceed further down the trail. She was uncertain about how well she would do climbing back up the steep trail.

She settled into the small campground near Dorsey Spring, prepared to wait while her companion explored further. Minutes passed, then an hour was gone. She heard a brief rustling in the brush and looked up to see a man walking toward her.

She would later describe him as having a dark complexion with dark hair. She noted his skin was dirty as if he had been camping for some time. He began to talk with her and she briefly answered his questions. As the minutes ticked by, she became more uncomfortable. Here she was, alone with a man she did not know. He became more animated, edging closer to her.

She glanced down the trail, hoping for sight of her companion returning to her. He did not come. She told the stranger that she must go in search of him. At that moment, he grabbed her arm.

"Don't go! I'm not done talking to you."

In panic, she pulled away from him.

"I have to find my partner," she insisted. She turned to flee. Just then her hiking partner emerged above the rim. He quickly understood her position and ran forward. The man disappeared into the brush.

"Are you all right?"

"No! Where were you?" she asked. "That guy was scaring me. He wouldn't let me go."

They made their way just over a mile up to the trail head and reported the incident to the Forest Service in Flagstaff.

What was the man doing in the canyon? Was he involved in illegal activity?

The Forest Service wanted to question this individual

and began to actively look for him. Illegal plots of marijuana have been planted throughout remote regions of our national forests in the last couple of decades. Often, a person down on his luck or here by illegal entry is hired to guard the plot. The Forest Service questioned whether this man may have been guarding an illegal crop.

Personnel from the Coconino Forest Service alerted the Bureau of Alcohol, Tobacco and Firearms (ATF) that there might be an illegal crop within the upper reaches of Sycamore Canyon. In the weeks following the incident, Jay noticed a helicopter flying over the canyon but gave very little thought to their purpose.

A month later, he woke to the bore end of a rifle in his face and the verbal command to come out from his shelter. Jay was not a stranger to the actions of law enforcement. He moved very slowly, telling the men that he would get dressed and come out to talk with them. He emerged to find officers of the ATF and the Forest Service, armed with semi-automatic rifles and pistols. Their faces were grim. He knew they were not fooling around.

Jay did not have an illegal crop of marijuana. He explained to the officers his purpose for living in the canyon, away from society's influence. In disbelief they stared at his camp, at the tarps and tent that covered the wood poles, at the stone fireplace and the cached supplies. Just how long had this guy been living here?

Camping is not illegal in the national forest but campers may stay in one location no longer than 14 days. Campers may not erect a semi-permanent structure. Gazing at his camp, the officers became aware that Jay had erected a semi-permanent dwelling and had lived in this location for months, maybe years. They arrested him.

However, they began to admire the camp, speculating over how this would be a great place for a little time off from the stress of their duties. They explained that they had spotted him from the helicopter as he was sitting on a rock.

"Hey, man," one said. "I feel bad that we have to kick you out of here. My boss told me I had to do this!"

"Well, my boss must have gotten hold of your boss and told him it was time for me to move," Jay responded.

The group climbed out of the canyon and Jay took up residence in the county jail. He was facing a short term for breaking federal laws as well as a fine. The Forest Service returned to Sycamore Canyon, dismantling his camp and hauling his possessions out of the canyon on mules. The accumulation of five years, including 200 books, filled two trucks. The ranger in charge contacted Jesse and arranged to deliver the load to his home on Elm Street. They arrived with a detailed list of every item removed from the canyon. Jesse signed for the load and began storing Jay's possessions in his garage. Jay was grateful and a bit in awe of the dedication of the men and women of the Forest Service.

When he was released, he returned to Flagstaff under a lifetime order barring him from ever camping or otherwise taking up residence in the Coconino National Forest.

He remained undeterred from living alone away from society and the company of man. Jay thought he might give the Gila National Forest a try. He would look for a place hidden from the patrols of Forest Service personnel where he might resume his study and lead a solitary life. He spent that summer camping and hiking through the Gila Wilderness.

In the fall, he returned to Flagstaff and the home shared with Bonnie Estes and Jesse Sandivir. Bonnie still owned the house in the cinder hills behind Sunset Crater National Monument. Now, she had heard that the building had been vandalized and windows broken.

She asked a friend to check on the structure for her. Jay overheard the conversation. He had nothing else going on and volunteered to ride along with the friend. It was one of those life altering moments as they arrived to find the structure mostly intact. One corner of the house was near to collapse but the remainder of the house was intact.

To imagine this structure, think of a three bedroom stick-built house with the walls a single width of board between the elements outside and the interior. A portion of the wood floor had collapsed in the front room and desert creatures were free to enter the structure from the crawl space below. No electricity, no running water - just a building ravaged by the elements and vandals. The structure was mostly sound. Jay returned to town and made Bonnie an offer.

"If I fix the damage to the house, will you allow me to live there as the caretaker?"

Bonnie could not say *yes* fast enough.

Jay repaired the corner of the building by replacing broken beams and a section of the roof. He replaced a portion of the floor and added sheet rock to the walls of the front

room. Along with the kitchen, this would be his living space. He boarded up the hallway that extended beyond the living room and left the other rooms unfinished. And then, he began to scavenge.

The area around the home was divided into lots that have been sold and resold. Some have structures that have been abandoned as the owners became discouraged living off the grid. They have simply walked away from whatever home they managed to construct or tow to their lot.

Some owners have stayed and thrive off the grid. There were several well-kept cabins in the area. Jay explored the abandoned dwellings. He found a broken mirror and soon fashioned a collage on the wall opposite the front window.

Broken shards formed a trunk with branches reaching to the ceiling.

He installed a wood stove out of a fifty-gallon barrel with the stove pipe extending up through the ceiling. Near the stove he placed a cot, covered by a bright quilt. He found an old chair and placed it next to a bookcase. An ancient rug covered the floor beneath his reading nook. Several small tables gave him working space.

On the far end of the house was the kitchen, one step down from his living space. A long L-shaped counter held a sink. A three-gallon cooler with a spigot hung over the sink, providing running water at the turn of a handle. Next to the cooler, was a small propane refrigerator and a hot plate where he could heat his meals.

Turning back toward the living room a visitor would find the wall between the two rooms hung with pots, skillets and utensils, all within easy reach as they hung from nails pounded into the wall. At one end of the kitchen, beyond the short end of the counter, Jay created a studio with the afternoon light pouring through a small window. Like any artist's studio, pots held an array of brushes and tubes of oil paints crowded the shelves. At the other end of the kitchen,

more shelves held several batteries, powered by solar panels that Jay had painstakingly acquired to give him electricity off the grid. There were three more rooms to the house, unfinished, that served as storage.

And then, there was the outhouse! The house had a bathroom that had not been functional for years. Sinks and showers require plumbing and running water. Neither of these were easily available. Jay preferred his outhouse, constructed out of an old refrigerator with a view of juniper and pinyon pine woodland. The door and insulation had been stripped away with the frame placed over a pit. It seemed to me that making a call to the outhouse in warm weather would have been fine, but during the winter, especially on a bitter cold night with the wind howling, the walk would have been a bit extreme!

Jay now lived in a home with a roof over his head. He could be warm and relatively comfortable. He began to express his artistic talent inside and out. Sculptures of recycled wire sprouted from the ground in a broad circle around his front door. Animals skulls and colored rocks were embedded in rusting metal parts. A cow skull covered in bright beads hung on one front corner. Flower pots were filled with an assortment of items that Jay scavenged from his long walks. Small benches created room to sit a while with an old awning extending from the front of the house. Inside, more recycled art lay on crates and tables from thrift stores or scavenging. He bought paint and canvas to once again create colorful paintings. He sold a few paintings.

One painting showed two children, hand in hand, peering into a small clearing in the forest bringing memories of the old Hansel and Gretel fairy tale. In a savage turn, another painting showed two bare feet pierced with cracked pipes releasing a flood of blood to pool along the lower edge of the canvas. I suspected that this painting was out of his astonishment at the generosity of God's gift of life. Other paintings were darker and more disturbing. Those came earlier out of a very dark place.

Two of my favorites were portraits, one of Thomas Merton, the other of a local artist with shoulder-length wavy gray hair. One glance and I remembered seeing the man on the streets of Flagstaff. Tucked into storage, nearly 70 paintings remained in the back rooms. Native Americans and Civil War generals stared from the boards. Bright scenes of the red rocks of Sedona mixed with portraits of friends and partners.

Jesse later recalled a large portrait that Jay created of him in shades of 'puke green' and purple. He had not been at all sure that this would work. Puke green! But he liked the final product.

Every couple of weeks, Jay turned the key in the ignition of an old truck and drove into town. Two weeks of grit slid down a shower drain while a load of clothes spun in a washing machine. He would eat a good meal and visit friends. At other times, he drove over to either Sunset Crater or Wupatki National Monument and visited the rangers, learning more about the high desert of Northern Arizona. He followed their suggestions, exploring the nearby cinder cones, ruins and small springs.

As he turned 62, he had a bit more cash at his disposal from Social Security but he still stuck to a tight discipline through the seasons. He read and thought carefully about what he was learning. By this point he had moved beyond the central concepts of Christianity to explore the theology of the Eastern Orthodox Church. While he did not join in the veneration of Mary or the Saints, he found the theology challenged him to meditate deeper than what he explored in our American-based denominations.

In 2014, he had been living in the house around five years. He believed that he had reached a point where it was not enough to simply read and study. He thought of all the people, the millions, without an intimate knowledge of a God who loved them. What was he doing to share the grace that God had shown him?

Was it not selfish to develop an intimate relationship with God and never share all the good that had emerged from his study?

When a rancher's cows wandered onto the property, Jay carved his own gate post before putting in a gate.

Jaybyrd

Chapter 7

Every month over a period of forty years Ken Mortenson walked into the local jail to talk with the inmates about God and what he believed God's word had to say to mankind.

In 2014, he received a call from his church, requesting that he talk with a woman about entering the jail as part of a Sunday Service program. Could Ken explain what was required for an individual who was interested in entering the jail to talk with the inmates as part of a Sunday service?

He explained that there was a process that applicants had to complete before they could obtain a badge and a time slot in the weekly schedule. They agreed to meet during the coffee hour between services at the church he attended. That Sunday, the caller met Ken at church and he began to give her the details of how to apply for an identification card. After several moments, she looked over at a man sidling up to join their conversation.

"Look, I'm not the one who wants to go into the jail," she said. "This is Jay Willison and he is interested in the jail ministry."

We still laugh about that moment. Did Jay wonder what

he would be getting into with this church guy? Was he concerned Ken would look down his nose at his full sleeve tats? Later that day, Ken, still laughing, told me of the incident.

"I ended up talking with a guy covered with tattoos who wants to help out in the jail."

"He's a Christian, right?" I asked.

"He seems to be from what he told me. At this point he wants to tag along and see how this all works."

As we got to know Jay, I thought about this man who wanted to see how this all worked - a man who spent years behind bars in prison now volunteering to be locked up with inmates to teach God's word? He certainly knew more about how the jail functioned than Ken ever would. Did he have a nervous twinge as the lock turned on the door of the room they were assigned? Did he settle into a comfort zone as he faced men who knew the system that he had once lived under?

When Ken enters the jail, he does not ask the men what they have done to be placed in prison. He took up that same principle with Jay. They would talk about Jesus' love for us, his sacrifice to bring us to God and the promise of eternal life at peace with God.

Over the next year, Ken and Jay, along with another man, entered the jail every two weeks to teach and share a little conversation with the inmates. The day came when Jay decided that he was comfortable with entering the jail on his own. Why should three men all enter one small room if he could split off and take another pod in the jail?

He asked for the pod with prisoners who had committed the most serious crimes. For the next two years, he taught the men that passed through the pod about what he had learned as if he 'were one beggar telling another where to find bread' - the bread of life.

The first Sunday Jay accompanied Ken to the jail, I invited him to join us for dinner before they entered the facility. Stepping out of the kitchen, I gazed up at a man a couple of inches over six foot with broad shoulders. He looked me straight in the eye and shook my hand as we said hello. Long sleeves covered the tats. He was clean shaven, his eyes clear and steady. When he smiled the muscles around his lips tightened and revealed even white teeth.

After that meal, Jay would come for another and in time seemed to feel comfortable dropping by an occasional visit on his trips into town. When he called to say he was coming, we dropped everything. This was a man I felt expected honesty and gave acceptance in return. He would not hesitate to question a statement but he did not condemn one's beliefs.

As I entered the front room to say hello, he would unwind from the chair in front of the wood stove. As I wrapped an arm around his waist in a hug, my head seem to only reach his chest. This was a big guy. His smile lit up his face and spread throughout the room.

He gave us no clue of the medical challenges that had begun to trouble him. Years of living rough were taking their toll. He freely admitted that years of using drugs had changed his brain and he did not know the extent of the damage.

One thing was obvious. He was overwhelmed by the love that God shows each of us. As he talked, he would sweep his arms out to either side as he mimiced the sound of a rocket exploding.

"Wow! This is just mind blowing." He exulted in the change that had come to his life.

I had been a Christian for 55 years at that point. To see his enthusiasm, his wonder at God's salvation stirred something old and cold within me.

Within months after meeting Jay, I lay in the hospital dying from the H1N1 flu virus with both pnuemococcyl and bacterial pneumonia. Jay, along with many others prayed fervently for my healing. After my recovery, Jay seemed to take on a new role in checking up on us. Ken was well into his 70s and starting to feel the years that had passed.

Ken had been out to Jay's home in the high desert near Sunset Crater. From his description, I was very curious about how this man lived off the grid and about the house that sheltered him. I was in the process of writing a book about the springs of Arizona. I asked Jay if I could interview him and he agreed. We settled on meeting at his home over barbequed steak. We would bring dinner.

Jay did not have a propane-powered grill. Instead, he pointed to a set of cement rings. The men stacked wood in the rings and lit the fire. When the flames were reduced to glowing coals, the steak grilled in just a few minutes. As I took the first bites of the meal, I hummed in appreciation of the rich flavor of the meat.

No mail service along this dirt track but Jay had a mailbox all his own.

"Is it good?" Jay asked, looking amused at my humming.

I nodded enthusiastically as my mouth filled with the warm juice of the beef.

After dinner, I began firing questions at Jay and he often struggled to recall the correct sequence of events from years earlier. When darkness settles in to the high desert, the high evening becomes quite cool. Jay excused himself and returned a moment later, pulling on a flannel shirt that was more holes than shirt. I had never seen a shirt in such sad shape.

"Jay, that shirt belongs in the rag bag," I muttered.

And then I clapped a hand over my mouth, realizing my disrespect for his clothing. I suspected he bought his clothing from the thrift stores in town. He barely had enough to survive on and a new shirt was not in the future.

How does one apologize for such a callous remark? Buying a new shirt would just rub his face in the economic gulf between us. I have sewn many flannel shirts over the years and the only apology that would suffice was to make Jay a new shirt. A shirt that would fit him properly. He had complained that most shirts were tight across the shoulders and the sleeves too short. I spent the evening, as questions and answers flowed, carefully considering his size. Broad shoulders, check. Long arms, check. Well muscled neck, check. His waist was trim but how trim? Would a large or extra-large pattern be called for? Did he have a favorite color?

He said he favored red.

Three weeks later, I asked him to come to dinner. I had measured and cut extra allowance, then sewn, carefully tucking and finishing each seam. I pulled out the shirt after dinner and offered it, even as I wondered if I were crazy to consider such a project. Jay graciously received the shirt but showed little enthusiasm.

Three hours later, my phone beeped with a text.

"Girl, you put a lot of work into this shirt. I love it!"

I received a couple more texts through the winter telling me how much he appreciated the shirt. His generosity of thankfulness warmed my heart. The next year I made another shirt.

The phone beeped with another message: "I love my shirts! I wash one while I wear the other."

In a society, where we have such abundance, I felt small considering what the two shirts meant to a man living off the grid in a cool climate.

After Jay was gone, many of his friends recalled his crazy texts celebrating dates on the calendar. Early in the morning our phones would begin to beep.

"Happy Easter, a glorious sunrise to celebrate the rays of resurrection stretching throughout this planet." Or, "Merry Christmas to all of you. Such a glorious day celebrating the birth of our Savior. I really appreciate your friendship."

The following year, Ken broke his bicep tendon. We depended on a wood stove to heat our home and had just begun to cut wood for the cold temperatures of the winter months ahead. Weeks later, Jay brought us a load of juniper he had cut. We never asked, he just knew the need and stepped in to help. These memories are the substance of friendship.

As we sat talking, Jay mentioned that his back was aching after cutting wood. He supplied the wood for the house he shared with Jesse and Bonnie each year. We all agreed that cutting wood was hard work. I hardly stopped to think about how physically fit this man was in the life he led off the grid. Arthritis happens and as the years pass, one learns to adapt.

We briefly heard from Jay again at Christmas. Then weeks passed with nothing from him. Concern began to nudge me. Why had we not heard from Jay? I suggested Ken call to check on him.

Several days passed and a text beeped on Ken's phone.

"Hey guys, thanks for checking up on me. I've been in the hospital for a month. Complication from non-Hodgkins cancer. I'll come by in a couple of days to check on you."

The word cancer tends to grab your attention. We both sent back texts inquiring how we could help. No reply.

Again, Ken sent a text.

"Jay, we would love to see you. Can we come by?"

When again, there was no response, I sent a text.

"Jay, we were out your way the other day and wanted to drop by. I wanted to check and see if you were home."

Jay was not home. He sent a text, saying he would love to see us at Bonnie's home, just down the road a couple of miles. We were to contact Bonnie about visiting hours. As I read the text, I knew the complications were bad.

A few days later, I sent another text.

"Jay, we want to come visit. Ken has tried to call Bonnie to set up a time. The phone is either busy or no one answers. I'm sorry. Please know we are thinking of you and talking with God."

We later learned that Jay was comatose at this point. There would be no further conversations between us about God in this lifetime.

Two days later, Jesse posted a note on facebook, announcing Jay's death. The messages began to roll in. We tried to call to learn more details. Jesse and Bonnie were overwhelmed by friends who loved Jay and were grieving the loss of their brother. They realized that a Memorial service would help to spread the covid virus, yet they wanted to answer the questions that were flying their direction. What had happened? How could Jay have died with so little warning?

Another announcement appeared on facebook, setting a date and time to explain what had happened and to lift a glass in honor of Jay Willison.

The soreness that Jay had complained of after cutting wood was not simply over-exertion. Returning home, he had gone to bed. Eventually, he could not even stand without help. After an initial visit to a general practitioner, a friend rolled him into the oncologist office. Jay learned that cancer had spread from his lymph nodes to his spine. The doctors were very positive about the prognosis.

"We can cure this. We'll start radiation immediately. You can beat this."

The conversation took a downturn.

"We have to tell you that the effects of the radiation may weaken the vertebrae in your neck. If these should shatter, you could be a quadriplegic the rest of your life."

That afternoon, others joined the three friends as they sat around discussing what Jay had learned from the oncologist and the expectations for treatment. Jay didn't say much. The shock of learning that he might never return to the life he had enjoyed, that he might become dependent on others was sinking in. When the friends left Jesse, Bonnie and Jay remained at the table.

"Well, fuck this!" Jay exclaimed.

He picked up the bottle of pain pills and poured the contents onto the table top. He picked up a spoon and methodically crushed the pills into a powder. Dumping the strong pain medication into a glass of water, he swallowed the contents. Jesse and Bonnie watched, saying little as they understood his decision to choose his own exit.

The three friends had all cared for Bonnie's mom

in her last weeks. They, in turn, discussed how they wished to be treated when their time came to die. Jesse and Bonnie understood what Jay had chosen.

They wheeled him out onto the porch where he could watch the wind stirring the pine trees, the long shadows stretching over the yard as the sun began to set. They captured a few final images with their cell phones. Jesse posted one of Jay with his left hand raised, saying goodbye. And they waited for him to nod off in a final descent into unconsciousness.

Darkness settled in. Jay remained conscious, watching the stars begin to appear. Jesse and Bonnie looked at each other uncomfortably. They did not feel right just leaving him out on the porch all night. They wheeled him into the house and got him settled in bed, expecting that he would stop breathing at some point during the night as the drugs slowed his rate of respiration.

Jay slept for 24 hours and then woke.

As he returned to consciousness, he seemed to accept the fact that he had not made his exit as he expected.

"Well, I guess God wasn't ready to take me yet."

Again, Jesse and Bonnie looked at each other and then at Jay.

"Jay, you just swallowed all the pain medication. What do we do now? I think we had better call Hospice."

Jay lasted nine days after his abortive attempt to end his life. God, in his mercy, took him in his own timing. Compared to the suffering of many, this was so quick with little time for all the people who would have said good-bye if they had known. Friends hugged and shared memories.

As I watched those gathered, I was struck by what a cross section of society had shown up to hear what had happened to Jay. To one side stood a tall cowboy, well over six feet with a stetson that added a couple more inches. A slender hispanic woman clutched his arm, dark eyes and dark hair with long bare legs that stretched down to platform wedges.

A woman in a wheelchair, accompanied by her two daughters sat near a man with long, gray hair aloft in the breeze. He stood to tell how he had met Jay and described how they had talked theology, sharing a common background in serving time for violating the laws of society. Another man in a Scottish kilt read a narrative, discribing his friendship with Jay.

Lance Israel stood to talk of their friendship over 15 years with Jay. Allison could not rise to speak, wiping away the tears as he described their last moments with Jay before he passed away.

Around the fringes of the crowd stood men and women well marked with Jay's artistry in the tat industry. Some stood back, as did I, watching the interaction. Others shared their memories. I do not know or would even guess whether many of these people shared the faith that had become such a central part of Jay's life. As I listened I understood that Jay had met each of these people where they were at in life. He did not look down his nose at their shortcomings, he simply joined them in conversation, listening to their struggles and dreams.

As such he crossed many boundaries that most Christians seem to think are impassable. We all build walls but Jay in his humanity cut windows in the walls, bringing the light of God into some very dark lives. As I considered this, I thought about my own reaction first to Jay and then to the people who gathered. Would I have been so open? I know many of them judged me as a church-going, self-righteous woman. They did not see my desire to talk with them about faith as Jay had done.

One woman in particular made me laugh. She described how Jay would begin to talk about some of the concepts he was considering. She described reaching the point where she would throw up her hands and exclaim, "Jay, I have no idea what you are talking about."

I wished that we could cross our boundaries and walk together, unafraid of the exterior appearance that may seem forbidding.

Such is the business of friendship, learned from a man who I've called a quotidian mystic. Jay was not a saint. I've tried to portray him, showing both his shortcomings as well as the vivid effect he had on other people. Ultimately, he lived a solitary life the last few years. When he chose to leave the solitude, he invested himself in others as he walked in the presence of God.

I've talked with Bonnie and Jesse since Jay died. They both talk about losing their center and wonder where they will be a year from now.

"I didn't realize how much balance he brought to Jesse and me," says Bonnie. He was the voice of wisdom, our security and comfort. "

A few years before he died, Margo McClellan drove out to his home to shoot a video she would call Bird Walk. When I wrote, asking permission to link the video to the manuscript, she wrote a description of Jay:

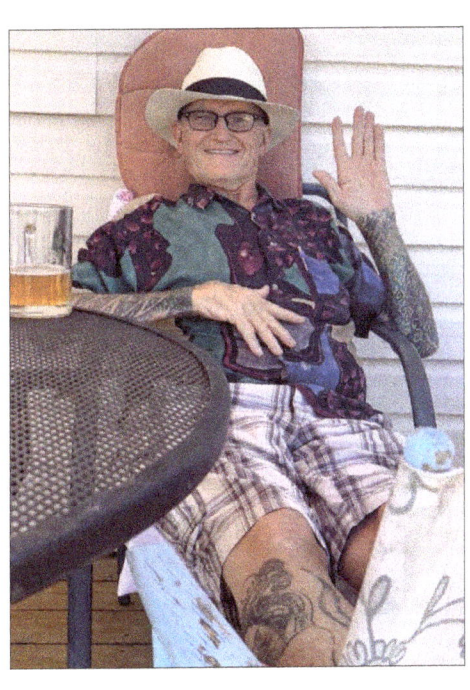

"I related to Jay immediately because I had been through some extremely dark years of my own ... having spoken with him and hearing his message of self-forgiveness, I have no doubt that his words and personality hovered in my unconscious and contributed to giving me the strength to pull myself out of the depths of despair before it was too late.

"I'd never met a tattooed, ex-drug addict, (outlaw biker), born-again Christian and incredibly talented artist who could quote Kierkegaard and light up the entire room with his smile. And I never will again."

Over the years Jay's style changed from impressionistic to a literal expression of what he witnessed.

Four Native American Portraits / Jaybyrd

Spirit Walking
A Study for the inmates of the Coconino County Jail
Jay 'Jaybyrd' Willison

Luke 1:29-35
But the angel said to her, "Do not be afraid, Mary; you have found favor with God. You will conceive and give birth to a son, and you are to call him Jesus. He will be great and will be called the Son of the Most High. The Lord God will give him the throne of his father David, and he will reign over Jacob's descendants forever; his kingdom will never end."

"How will this be," Mary asked the angel, "since I am a virgin?"

The angel answered, "The Holy Spirit will come over you, and the power of the Most High will overshadow you. So the holy one to be born will be called the Son of God."

When Christ the God-man entered time from eternity he was formed in human flesh through Mary by the power of the Holy Spirit. He was fully human and fully Divine yet his Divine characteristics were constrained or held back by his humaness. In this state of humaness he remained in complete harmony with his Father through the Holy Spirit. This was a harmony of knowledge and understanding whereby his human life was Spirit guided through time to fulfill that which as ordained from the beginning of time. This is why he is called the Son of God because he has always been and always will be united in this way. He is God the Son inseparable yet unconfused with God the Father and God the Holy Spirit. They are of the same substance yet they function together in complementing relationships of Divine Love. They all eternally converge into one another. This is why God is Love.

There are hundreds of prophesies concerning the coming of the Messiah which means the Anointed one. Anointed refers to his inseparable relationship with the Father through the Holy Spirit who will guide his human mission of setting us free from the bondage of sin and death. Through his Spirit guided humanity he brings us into spiritual birth, a new creation which culminates in a resurrected spirit body like Christ's. Through his human existence he transformed our human nature into one that is able to participate with the Holy Spirit.

Here are a few of those prophesies given through Isaiah concerning his inseparable union with the Holy Spirit. Isaiah spoke these prophesies about 700 years before Christ's entrance into time:

Isaiah 11:2 *"The Spirit of the Lord will rest on him –*
The Spirit of wisdom and of understanding,
the spirit of counsel and of might,
the Spirit of the knowledge and fear of the Lord –"

Isaiah 42:1 *"Here is my servant, whom I uphold,*
My chosen one in whom I delight;
I will put my Spirit on him,
and he will bring justice to the nations."

Isaiah 61:1 *"The Spirit of the Sovereign Lord is on me,*
because the Lord has anointed me
to proclaim good news to the poor.
He has sent me to bind up the brokenhearted,
to proclaim freedom to for the captives
and release from darkness for the prisoners."

Throughout Christ's life he was directed by his union with the Holy Spirit into spiritual knowledge and understanding harmonizing his humanity into spiritual harmony with the kingdom of God. By bringing himself into human form he became the first fully functional human being. By doing this he opens up our humanity to the ability to participate in spiritual harmony with the spiritual the kingdom of God. His spiritual understanding grew step by step throughout his life preparing him for his timeless task of setting us free. The Bible gives us a small glimpse into this:

> Luke 2:41-52 *Every year Jesus' parents went to Jerusalem for the Festival of the Passover. When he was twelve years old, they went up to the festival, according to the custom. After the festival was over, while his parents were returning home, the boy Jesus stayed behind in Jerusalem, but they were unaware of it. Thinking he was in their company, they traveled on for a day. Then they began looking for im among they relatives and friends. When they did not find him, they went back to Jerusalem to look for him. After three days they found him in the temple courts, sitting among the teachers, listening to them and asking them questions. Everyone who heard him was amazed at his understanding and his answers. When his*

parents saw him, they were astonished. His mother said to him, "Son, why have you treated us like this? Your father and I have been anxiously searching for you."

"Why were you searching for me?" he asked. "Didn't you know I had to be in my Father's house?" But they did not understand what he was saying to them.

Then he went down to Nazarath with them and was obedient to them. But his mother treasured all this things in her heart. And Jesus grew in wisdom and stature, and in favor with God and man."

Jesus Christ's whole life was different from any other human being that was ever born into this world. The difference? His whole person, mind, heart and soul was in living and active Spiritual harmony, through this harmonious relationship his growth and learning confirmed his spiritual path. His Teacher was the Holy Spirit living in him, the indwelling Spirit of love and harmony increasingly confirmed his love for his heavenly Father. Every experience, every conflict, every emotion, was in spiritual context (harmony) with his heavenly Father. His Spirit is the Spirit of his Father. His presence here on earth opened for humanity an unbroken harmony of spiritual thinking, acting and being *in* the world but not *of* the world. Jesus was in total oneness with the Holy Spirit, in total harmony with the will of God in order to spiritually engage the task of his life. When his ministry began at thirty years old he was baptized.

Matthew 3:16-17 *As soon as Jesus was baptized, he went up out of the water. At that moment heaven was opened, and he* (John the Baptist) *saw the Spirit of God descending like a dove and alighting on him. And a voice from Heaven said, "This is my Son, whom I love; with him I am well pleased."*

Christ's baptism in the waters of the Jordan River was an illustration from nature, a metaphor that reveals something far more, something unseen. The Bible is loaded with these analogies and metaphors, they speak of Spiritual realities. In fact, everything Jesus did and said were far more powerful and real than the signs he performed or the words spoke because he saw everything with the eyes of the Spirit living in him. Jesus did not see things in this world as we see them. His stories were from daily life in Palestine, they were bound by time and space yet they pointed to the eternal realm of the Spirit. The healing he did were acts that revealed spiritual truths. The miracles, the Words, the events of his life, his death, his resurrection broke open the prison door that divided our minds from the ability to see and participate in spiritual reality. His whole existence made it possible for us to participate, through him, in a new life powered by the same Spirit that directed his human existence. He is the door through whom we can enter the difference, a different life powered by the Holy Spirit.

Romans 6:8-10 *"Now if we died with Christ, we believe that we will also live with im. For we know that since Christ was raised from the dead, he cannot die again; death no longer has mastery over him. The death he died, he died to sin once for all; but the life he lives, he lives to God."*

I live out off the grid and recently it snowed pretty good for a few days. My neighbor was asked to help someone who was stuck, he took his four-wheel drive out and he became stuck, on level ground, not far from his house. He discovered he had a problem. In fact he had a few problems, he had no weight in the back to help give him traction, he had bald tires, but most of all, his four-wheel drive didn't work.

We all suffer from the same thing, we think we have it all figured out, we have everthing we could possibly need in life, a healthy body, a good mind, heart, soul, family, friends, we roll along tearing it up and then, BAM! We get stuck! In the first mud puddle, not a hill in sight.

When we are born we learn to get along in this insane crazy world hopefully with the help of family and friends to teach us how to feed ourselves, cloth ourselves, how to get along with people, go to school, get a job, work. Even if we know all the basics it doesn't mean it will work out all the time. The world is full of trouble physically, mentally and spiritually.

We love to blame everything for our trouble but the underlying reason for our breakdown isn't everybody else's fault or the weather or the mud - it is us, something deep down inside our nature, sin! Our sinful nature is irrational and foolish in fact the word sin means to go the wrong way, miss the mark, this is because we are spiritually blind and broken! We may be aware of spiritual things but we lack the power we need to gain traction.

What's really funny is that my friend already knew his 4WD didn't work, he knew his tires were bald, he lied to himself, he thought that somehow, perhaps through sheer willpower that things might work out just fine. Most of us know that we are broke but have no idea how to just stop! Get it together and get it fixed. The real trip is that there are tons of 'church folk' that are broke down too. Trying to drive their spiritual life on four flat tires. When one is in spiritual poverty it doesn't matter what one's life is like, human beings are all broke, even if you do well in the world and are getting along fine, with no genuine spiritual life the spiritual 4WD is broke and all it takes is one bad road trip to bring the illusion crashing down.

Ephesians 2:1-3 *As for you, you were dead in your transgressions and sins, in which you used to live when you followed the ways of this world and of the ruler of the kingdom of the air, the spirit who is now at work in those who are disobedient. All of us also lived among them at one them, gratifying the cravings of our flesh and following its desires and thoughts. Like the rest, we were by nature deserving of wrath."*

So, it seems that without our becoming united with the Spirit we remain broke, in fact the sinful mind thinks it's fine, everything is as it should be. I have everything I need to get along without God's help. This attitude is called the law of sin and death. We keep on doing the same meaningless things over and over, being content or thinking it will change, thinking we can do this, thinking we will make it through the ice and mud. The sinful mind is so full of pride that it would rather remain spiritually broken than to accept the gift of God's forgiveness and spiritual power in Christ.

The spiritual breakthrough comes when one is cleansed of sin and our sin driven nature powered by an irrational mind is put in check. To be born again is to put our sin and sinful life to death, daily, on the cross. With our sin and guilt nailed to the cross, and the power of a sinful nature held down, we are given a gift ! The same Spirit who raised Christ from the dead lives within us to help us learn how to see, hear and walk spiritually, slowly one awakens to understand the reality of this gift. This awakening shows us that there is now a difference. Spiritual truth reveals the futility of being 'without' a fully functional, spiritualized life.

> Romans 8:5-8 *Those who live according to the flesh have their minds set on what the flesh desires; but those who live in accordance with the Spirit have their minds set on what the Spirit desires. The mind governed by the flesh is hostile to God; it does not submit to God's law, nor can it do so. Those who are in the realm of the flesh cannot please God.*

This Spiritual walk means to participate in the gift of a spiritualized thinking. Learning to grow spiritually functional are areas of the mind, heart and soul. To be made alive spiritually is to have access to Truth, Goodness and Beauty which directs our mind, heart and soul into harmony with the will of God. Through Christ we have access to spiritual potency that gives power to our once 'broken' potentiality. Spiritual life means to 'walk' in context within the potency of Truth, Goodness and Beauty. This growing spiritual attitude rewires the way we function. Our inner structure is repaired and now we learn how to use our potentiality in harmony with spiritual potency, this activity for the Good! All of our faculties and abilities now are in the company of the concepts of the Spirit. Our teacher is the Holy Spirit.

> I Corinthians 2:10-14 *The Holy Spirit searches all things, even the deep things of God. For who knows a person's thoughts except their own spirit within them? In the same way no one knows the thoughts of God except the Spirit of God. What we have received is not the spirit of the world, but the Spirit who is from God, so that we*

may understand what God has freely given us. This is what we speak, not in words taught us by human wisdom but in words taught by the Spirit, explaining spiritual realities with Spirit-taught words. The person without the Spirit does not accept the things that come from the Spirit of God but considers them foolishness, and cannot understand them because they are discerned only through the Spirit.

To be born again opens a new path into the land of the spiritually living. The kingdom of God opens to those who seek to see with the Spiritual eyes of faith. Through faith one begins the work of seeking out and coming to understand the language of the kingdom. This work enables us to shift into our new spiritual gear (new creation). Jesus put it simply like this:

John 3:3-5 *Jesus replied, "Very truly I tell you, no one can see the kingdom of God unless they are born again."*

"How can someone be born when that are old?" Nicodemus asked. "Surely they cannot enter a second time into their mother's womb to be born!"

Jesus answered, "Very truly I tell you, no one can enter the kingdom of God unless they are born of water and the Spirit. Flesh gives birth to flesh, but the Spirit gives birth to spirit."

In order to 'see' spiritually, one must become a spiritually alive human being which is by faith. To believe in the Word of Christ is the work of faith, which gives birth to our spiritual nature, this is the gift needed to awaken the mind, heart and soul into a spiritual context. With the awakening of this new birth we begin to see what was unseen and to hear and understand spiritual words, which are incomprehensible without faith. It's a new way of life and it takes a lot of work because we are still in conflict by our old ways of life but now we have the difference.

> John 6:63 *"Jesus said; 'The Spirit gives life; the flesh counts for nothing. The words I have spoken to you - they are full of the Spirit and life.'"*
>
> Romans 10:17 The Apostle Paul tells us, *"Consequently, faith comes from hearing the message, and the message is heard through the word about Christ."*
>
> Hebrews 11:1 *"Now faith is the substance of things hoped for, the evidence of things not seen."*
>
> 2 Corinthians 4:16-18 *"Therefore, we do not lose heart. Though outwardly we are wasting away, yet inwardly we are being renewed day by day. For our light and momentary troubles are achieving for us an eternal glory that far outweighs them all. So we fix our eyes not on what is seen, but on what is unseen, since what is seen is temporary, but what is unseen is eternal."*

Faith open the way to the realm of the Kingdom. To function in this realm we need spiritual food. This spiritual food is the Word of God. Through these words we are increasingly able to understand. This renewed mind awakens the heart and soul into a new dimension. This new context or harmony requires some getting used to because it offers a new way of looking at the situations of life. This is realized through the context of faith. Faith makes spiritual things clear to a mind that is used to doing things alone, without any spiritual help. We now enter into the work of God who begins to build in us a mind that is in spiritual harmony with Him.

> Colossians 3:1-2 *"Since, then, you have been raised with Christ, set your hearts on things above, where Christ is, seated at the*

right hand of God. Set your minds on things above, not on earthly things."

So to begin this 'work' is to learn how to prepare one's mind for spiritual thinking, it takes work because the same mind we used to think of destructive and meaningless things is still in the habit of blinding us to the real Truth. The new spirit mind challenges the old ways of thinking. It is a war, our weapons are Truth where by we discover true Goodness that brings Beauty into our life. Grace is the power of the Spirit at work within, the power and potency we need to begin to do the good we come to know and understand.

Philippians 4:8-9 (Ampified) *"Finally, believers, whatever is true, whatever is honorable and worth of respect, whatever is right and confirmed by God's word, whatever is pure and wholesome, whatever is lovely and brings peace, whatever is admirable and of good repute; if there is any excellence, if there is anything worth of praise, think continually on these things (center your mind on them, and implant them in your heart.)"*

To begin this fight, the 'good fight' is to begin to challenge our thinking with these things. What do you 'allow' yourself to think about? With the help of God's Spirit our mind can recognize our old destructive habits, we see their meaninglessness and reject their influence! Replacing the old thought, forcibly, and begin to build a structure of spiritually oriented Truth.

Galations 5:16-21 *"So I say, walk by the Spirit, and you will not gratify the desires of the flesh. For the flesh desires what is contrary to the Spirit, and the Spirit what is contrary to the flesh. They are in conflict with each other, so that you are not to do whatever you want.*

But if you are led by the Spirit, you are not under the law.

The acts of the flesh are obvious: sexual immorality, impurity and debauchery; idolatry, and witchcraft; hatred, discord, jealousy, fits of rage, selfish ambition, dissensions, factions and envy; drunkenness, orgies and the like. I warn you, as I did before, that those who live like this will not inherit the kingdom of God."

The faculties of the soul have been out of gear for so long that they have been forced to function on meaningless things like the ones above. Our instruments or the operators of the soul are freedom, desire, reason, intentions, discernment (judgement), ambition and other aspects of the will. These instruments either work for us or against us, they need something to do so they will focus on whatever we given them to do. So we must begin to develop spiritual habits in order to get them working on things that matter, then our will shall start working the way it was intended, spiritually! Without a spiritual life these functions remain broken.

Romans 6:12-14 *"Therefore do not let sin reign in your mortal body so that you obey its evil desires. Do not offer any part of yourself to sin as an instrument of wickedness, but rather offer yourselves to God as those who have been brought from death to life; and offer every part of yourself to him as an instrument of righteousness. For sin shall no longer be your master, because you are not under the law, but under grace."*

Our helper, the Holy Spirit, (John 14:26 & 16:7) who is living in us, helps us understand the Word of God and we begin to see the path. To prayerfully read the scriptures is like putting tread on our tires, it gives solid concepts to our mind, heart and soul for spiritual traction. These Spirit-powered words helps us to recognize and understand the right way to go. The right way, at the right time, with the right intention, for the right reason, the right words, the right thinking, the right gear. This is what righteousness means. To act in harmony with the will of God. To be in fellowship with the Father is to be in fellowship with righteousness. This righteousness starts to produce its Spiritual fruit in our lives!

> Galations 5:22-25 *"But the fruit of the Spirit is love, joy, peace, forbearance, kindness goodness, faithfulness, gentleness and self-control. Against such things there is no law. Those who belong to Christ Jesus have crucified the flesh with its passions and desires. Since we live by the Spirit, let us keep in step with the Spirit."*

Notice how these fruits flow from a love, they all are relationship, and these fruits are principles of love that work in every relationship whether they are spiritual, personal, social. They are life giving fruits and as they grow in one's life they increase and grow stronger.

> 2 Peter 1:3-9 *"His divine power has given us everything we need for a godly life through our knowledge of him who called us by his own glory and goodness. Through these he has given us his very great and precious promises, so that through them you may participate in the divine nature, having escaped the corruption in the world caused by evil desires.*
>
> *For this very reason, make every effort to add to your faith goodness; and to goodness, knowledge, and to knowledge, self-control; and to self-control, perseverance; and to perseverance; godliness; and to godliness, mutual affection; and to mutual affection, love. For if you possess these qualities in increasing measure, they will keep you from being ineffective and unproductive in your knowledge of our Lord Jesus Christ. But whoever does not have them is nearsighted and*

blind, forgetting that they have been cleansed from their past sins."

To have the Holy Spirit living in us is to participate in the divine nature of Christ which is love. In this presence of Christ, the mind guided by the Spirit's influence grows within us. Our heart begins to reflect the nature of Christ in the transforming activity of our soul bringing light into every other relationship of our lives. It is the walk of faith. The Spirit Way!

> *Brothers and sisters, whatever is true,*
> *whatever is noble, whatever is right,*
> *whatever is pure, whatever is lovely,*
> *whatever is admirable—*
> *if anything is excellent*
> *or praiseworthy*
> *—think about such things.*
> Philippians 4:8

www.ingramcontent.com/pod-product-compliance
Lightning Source LLC
Chambersburg PA
CBHW051601010526
44118CB00023B/2778